Shooting Outdoor Videos

Shooting Outdoor Videos

by Donald C. Steffens

RAGGED MOUNTAIN PRESS
CAMDEN, MAINE

Published by Ragged Mountain Press

10 9 8 7 6 5 4 3 2 1

Library of Congress Cataloging-in-Publication Data
Steffens, Donald C.
Shooting outdoor videos / by Donald C. Steffens
p. cm.
Includes bibliographical references and index.
ISBN 0-87742-325-3 (paper)—ISBN 0-87742-350-4 (hard)
1. Cinematography—Amateurs' manuals. 2. Outdoor photography—Amateurs' manuals. 3. Camcorders—Amateurs' manuals. 4. Video recording—Amateurs' manuals. I. Title.
TR896.5.S74 1993
778.59'92—dc20 93-505
CIP

Questions regarding the content of this book should be addressed to:

Ragged Mountain Press
P.O. Box 220
Camden, ME 04843

Questions regarding the ordering of this book should be addressed to:

TAB Books
A Division of McGraw-Hill, Inc.
Blue Ridge Summit, PA 17294
1-800-233-1128

A portion of the profits from the sale of each Ragged Mountain Press book is donated to an environmental cause.

Shooting Outdoor Videos is printed on 60-pound Renew Opaque Vellum, an acid-free paper which contains 50 percent recycled waste paper (preconsumer) and 10 percent postconsumer waste paper.

Photos on pages 38, 39, and 69 by Chris Townsend
Photo on page 58 by David Schaefer
Photo on page 52 by Gael Steffens
All other photos by Donald Steffens
Illustrations by Dawn Peterson
Printed by R. R. Donnelly, Harrisonburg, VA
Design by Patrice Rossi
Production and page layout by Janet Robbins
Edited by Jonathan Eaton, Kathy Newman, and Pamela Benner

To Gaelie, who did so
much more work than she
can ever receive credit for.
Without her support,
encouragement, and love,
I could not live happily,
much less have written
this book.

CONTENTS

INTRODUCTION

Home videos today are much like home movies were to earlier generations of film users. In the 1940s and 1950s, it seemed everyone owned a small motion-picture camera and was out in the backyard shooting footage of family and friends at play. Even family pets were captured forever on the celluloid frames of motion-picture films. The Eastman Kodak Company was the undisputed leader in this field, and from its manufacturing headquarters in Rochester, New York, came frequent, glowing reports of ever-improving products that would soon revolutionize the home-movie market. Even the encroachment of television—with its ability to show live action, combining both sound and picture—failed to diminish the enthusiasm most people had for film. Film was portable, inexpensive, and reproduced color. Television images were still black and white. TV cameras were huge, bulky things, prohibitively expensive for the average consumer, and videotape was still an experimental product confined to professional broadcast studios. Home movies on film would be around for a long, long time.

Of course, television and its ally, videotape, quickly grew and prospered beyond anyone's expectations, and the technology moved out of the broadcast studio and into the consumer marketplace. Film was "out," except for commercial film operations; video was "in." Today, people still have great interest in making home movies of their favorite pastimes. Kids, grown-ups, and pets are still directed to perform by someone behind the viewfinder, and the flexibility of the new video equipment makes home movies more appealing than ever before. The really good news for this generation of moviemakers is that, in many ways, video is like the old-fashioned home films, only better. Video is easier and faster. A viewable product is instantly available. You don't have to wait weeks for film to be developed at a remote lab and mailed back.

Video is a growing field. It's already the accepted medium for home entertainment. In the years ahead, video will become more popular, and right now there doesn't appear to be any practical limit to how far it can go. The nice thing about getting into video now is that you're getting in almost on the ground floor. You and this amazing technology can grow together.

Although it's a new and expanding field, video borrows heavily from the fields of movie filming and still photography. Many of the same basic techniques and principles are used in all three fields. So even if you're new to videography, you might know more about it than you think.

And there's more good news for the beginner: Just as the physical movements and skills developed for one sport can often be transferred to another, the same is true for shooting videos. The basic techniques and guidelines you use in shooting videos of one sport or outdoor activity can be applied to another, and yet another, until they become habit—second nature, really—and you're able to use the camera well in a variety of settings.

It's on this concept of an interrelationship among activities that this book is based. In simple terms, this is a book about the outdoors and how you can make video movies that capture all your fun and outdoor adventures.

Use this book as a sampler of various techniques and principles of video production that apply to all outdoor activities. No matter what your interest, whether it is boating, fishing, tennis, birdwatching, travel, relaxing with sun, sand, and surf at the beach, or just watching others at play, the basic lessons in these pages will help you shoot better, maybe even professional-looking videos in the varied and demanding conditions found outdoors.

Although this is a beginner's book, the emphasis is on learning some of the tricks and techniques practiced by professionals, and then adapting them to the equipment we can buy at regular consumer outlets. As your skill at shooting videos improves and your interest in this field grows, you'll find bigger and better pieces of equipment to satisfy your every need. Your initial needs, however, are basic.

The eye and imagination of the videographer account for the success of any video movie. Whether a video sequence is pleasant to watch, or exciting or beautiful, depends in great measure on how you saw the scene and then interpreted it. A video camera lens, however expensive and versatile, does nothing more creative than open electronically when you push a button, admitting a controlled amount of light energy that activates the videotape in the camera's body. You are the controlling factor, the creative force in this equation. You must select the scene, consider the amount and source of light falling on your subject, calculate how the final series of pictures will look, and then act creatively to move into the best position to make the camera record your vision. That process requires work, but it can be a great source of fun, and the rewards of seeing your interpretation of the scene played back through your own television set are even greater. Delighting your audience with your videos brings more rewards.

It's truly a creative process, but there are some well-worn paths to follow. It's the goal of this book to show you those paths.

Shooting Outdoor Videos

CHAPTER ONE

The Standard Package

Your eyes and imagination are the twin keys to unlocking the secrets and mysteries to producing good videos. How you see things and how your mind interprets what you see determine the final product. Combined, they can be considered the soul of any video project. Yet it is also true that better equipment yields better results if everything else is equal. So, decide how much you're willing to spend on any video component, and then strive for the best value for your dollar.

The video camera itself is the heart of the system. It's clearly the most important piece of video equipment you'll have. It's also likely to be the most expensive item on your shopping list, so consider carefully before buying. Today's sophisticated video cameras and recorders pack an amazing array of electronic features, even on the amateur level, that professional photographers and moviemakers just a few years ago could only dream about. Now they're available to everyone. Zoom lenses, variable-speed shutters, automatic controls with manual overrides, and many other features make video cameras so flexible and forgiving that even a beginner can achieve good results using some of the tricks and tips that others have pioneered.

You'll first want to decide what features you feel you must have, and then consider some of the additional features to make your videos more enjoyable. The heft of your pocketbook might well determine the extras. Don't base your purchase solely on the extra features offered, because many of them are unnecessary to basic moviemaking and might, in fact, complicate your work later on when it's time to edit your story. Concentrate instead on the quality of the camera and the lens, the sturdiness of the tape transport system, and the durability of the camera housing. Whether you buy from a retail store, a discounter, or a mail-order catalog, look for a good combination of price and warranty, but consider that video cameras are durable, and you're more likely to buy a replacement because you've been seduced by new technology than because your current camera breaks.

In the early days of video, just a few years ago, video cameras were manufactured separately from the videocassette recorders (VCRs). As the technology improved, the electronics were miniaturized and manufacturers were able to combine both the camera and the videocassette recorder into the same package. The result: the camera-recorder, or *camcorder* (for purposes of this book, however, I'll use the generic term *video camera*). This is a remarkable piece of electronic equipment for the home market. The built-in VCR is now a standard feature on equal footing with a good lens; even the most economical video camera has these two features. Additional bells and whistles are always available for a price, of course, and each year the list of options and standard features grows.

THE LANGUAGE OF VIDEO

People who work around computers have developed a complex, specialized language of their own, commonly called computerese. To the first-time computer user, it's a difficult, foreign language. Like all foreign languages, computerese must be studied and learned before you can communicate effectively with those who use it.

A similar situation exists in the world of video because most video devices are, in fact, computers, or at least contain computer components in their design. They're all plastic boxes filled with silicon computer chips, so you can be sure computer jargon isn't far behind. A page of promotional literature for a leading video system brags about its recording features, which "increase horizontal resolution" by an upward shift of the "luminance carrier" while expanding the "frequency deviation." Being not very technically minded, I have only an approximate idea what that means. Fortunately, my lack of electronic engineering knowledge in no way detracts from my enjoyment of shooting videos. In this book, therefore, I've tried to stay away from engineering and computer jargon, concentrating instead on easy-to-understand terms and explanations. You want to shoot videos, not repair microchips. If you need an occasional reminder of what a term means, refer to the Glossary at the end of the book. (Throughout this book you'll sometimes see words in *italic type*; this is a key to let you know these words are also defined in the Glossary.)

You'll be relieved to know that since video is so new, it's developing its language slowly. Much of the working language of video is similar to that of photography and moviemaking, so you've probably already been exposed to some of it. We speak of video cameras being equipped with certain kinds of lenses and having variable shutter speeds and built-in viewfinders. We even speak of filming an event, when we should call it videotaping. And a videographer can be called a photographer without offending any but the purist.

Almost everyone has had some experience with still cameras, and a basic video camera is just as easy to use as one of today's new automatic-exposure film cameras. Any familiarity you have with the terms and techniques of photography will be of great help in understanding and using video.

HOW A VIDEO CAMERA WORKS

The video camera collects light from the subject and transmits it through the lens where it is formed into an image. The visible image registers on a *charge-coupled device (CCD),* also known as an *imaging chip.* This semiconductor chip contains as many as 400,000 silicon photodiodes, which convert the light into electrical impulses that activate the magnetic coating on the videotape via the video recording heads. Sound waves picked up by the microphone are also transformed and recorded on the tape. At the same time, the audio and video electronic impulses excite sensors in the *viewfinder,* which is actually a tiny black-and-white TV set attached to the camera. (A few models have color viewfinders, but these can make it harder to determine when you're in sharp focus.) You are, in fact, watching a television picture of your subject. Everything takes place electronically. The only mechanical action is the videotape moving in the tape cartridge from one spool to the other.

When you play back a videotape on which something has been recorded, the process is reversed. The playback machine changes electrical energy to light and sound patterns that eventually reach your eyes and ears through a TV monitor and are perceived as faithful images of the real thing.

VIDEO FORMATS

It would be nice if there were just one standard video format that all manufacturers followed. But this is the real world and every manufacturer thinks its ideas are better than the rest. So, each developed its own specialized form of videotape and accompanying equipment. What we poor consumers end up with is a dizzying array of models in a number of formats, most of which are not compatible with each other. Adding to the confusion is the fact that a small number of Japanese manufacturers produce almost all the models, including not only their own brands (the various Sony, JVC, Hitachi, and Matsushita models), but also the virtually identical models sold by other companies. Again, the safest approach is to sort through the available formats and features, decide what you want, and then look for a good combination of price and warranty.

Basically, there are two families of video formats: *VHS* and *8mm.* (The old BETA format is so rarely used today, and is no longer even available in stores, that it doesn't warrant discussing.) These formats are not compatible: VHS tapes will only work in VHS machines; 8mm tapes will only work with compatible 8mm equipment (although a tape *can* be dubbed, or copied, from an 8mm camcorder onto a VHS tape in a VHS VCR). Each has its advantages and disadvantages.

The VHS Family

There are four formats in the VHS family: *VHS*, compact VHS (called *VHS-C*), super or high-band VHS (called *S-VHS* or *H-VHS*), and compact super VHS (called *S-VHS-C*). In all of these, the audio signal is recorded separately from the video signal (on a track along the edge of the tape), and so can be replaced on the original tape by using the audio-dub feature of the video camera in playback mode. Since the original soundtrack is lost, however, this feature is of limited usefulness for outdoor videos. You might use it to introduce music during a lingering panoramic setup shot or for some "follies" footage of beginning downhill skiers, but a little goes a long way. In the long run, the absence of ambient noise in an outdoor video creates an artificial effect. On the downside, recording the audio signal on a narrow, edge-of-the-tape track means that the soundtrack quality of VHS falls short of 8mm. In some cameras, particularly S-VHS, this is countered with a separate sound recording head for high-fidelity sound, but at the cost of an increase in camera size. Stereo video cameras are also available, but be aware that if stereo sound is your objective, every component in the record/playback chain must be stereo, including your TV monitor. Even then the effect is diluted without widely separated speakers.

VHS

VHS is the oldest and, until recently, the most popular format. For one thing, it's compatible with the VCRs most people have in their living rooms—most of the movies you can rent at your local video outlet are produced on VHS. Also, the full-size videotapes can record for 2 to 3 hours at normal speed—plenty of time to record enough scenes to edit into an interesting movie.

The picture quality is generally good for home recordings, though it deteriorates somewhat when the tape is duplicated. Because a VHS tape is large, however, the tape transport system, and thus the camera itself, tends to be bulky. While some of us might enjoy the sturdy, steady feel of an 8-pound camera resting on our shoulder, others don't. That's one reason why the 8mm format has become so popular and why VHS-C was developed.

Compact VHS (VHS-C)

The compact version of VHS is virtually the same as the full-size version, except that everything is smaller, including the tape cartridge (the width of the tape is the same, but the length is shorter so that it fits in a smaller cartridge). The tapes in VHS-C have only about a 30- to 45-minute running time on standard play. You can play them on a standard VHS VCR by means of a cassette adapter (available for

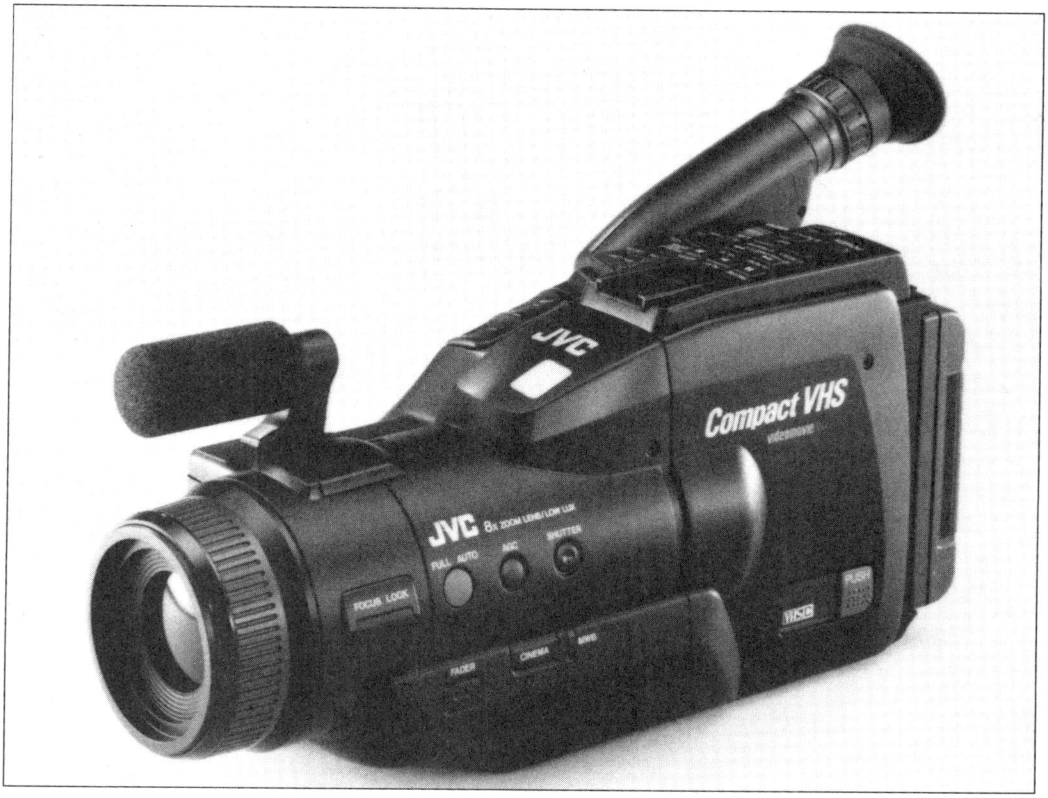

Compact VHS or VHS-C. (Courtesy JVC)

a modest investment if it doesn't come with your camera), or by leaving the tape in the video camera and plugging the camera directly into a TV set. Some newer VCRs accommodate both full-size and compact tapes.

The picture quality is as good as VHS, but the real advantage to VHS-C is that the cameras are small, lightweight, and easy to tote around. The biggest drawback, again, is the short playing time.

Super VHS (S-VHS)

Super (or high-band) VHS, an electronically enhanced version of VHS, has outstanding resolution, almost double the previous standards. In fact, it approaches commercial broadcast standards with approximately 400 lines of horizontal resolution, as opposed to early VHS models, which might have reached 150 to 300 lines. This means much clearer pictures, more realistic and vivid color, and less color fade and breakup of the picture when the tape is copied or edited.

Here's where incompatibility rears its ugly head. Although you can use standard VHS tapes in S-VHS machines (including cameras and VCRs), you can't play S-VHS tapes on a standard VHS VCR. You can, however, play them from the playback or VCR portion of the S-VHS video camera via cables to your TV set. An S-VHS tape played from the camera via standard cables to an ordinary television set will give much richer, sharper images than a VHS tape.

Compact super VHS (S-VHS-C)

S-VHS-C is the super version of the compact VHS format. Like S-VHS, S-VHS-C offers sharp, clear pictures. The tapes (which are the same as the S-VHS tape, only shorter) run for about 30 to 45 minutes, and you can play them in your S-VHS VCR with a cassette adapter, or directly from the camera to the TV set via connecting cables. As with the S-VHS format, though, the S-VHS-C videotapes won't work in standard VHS VCRs.

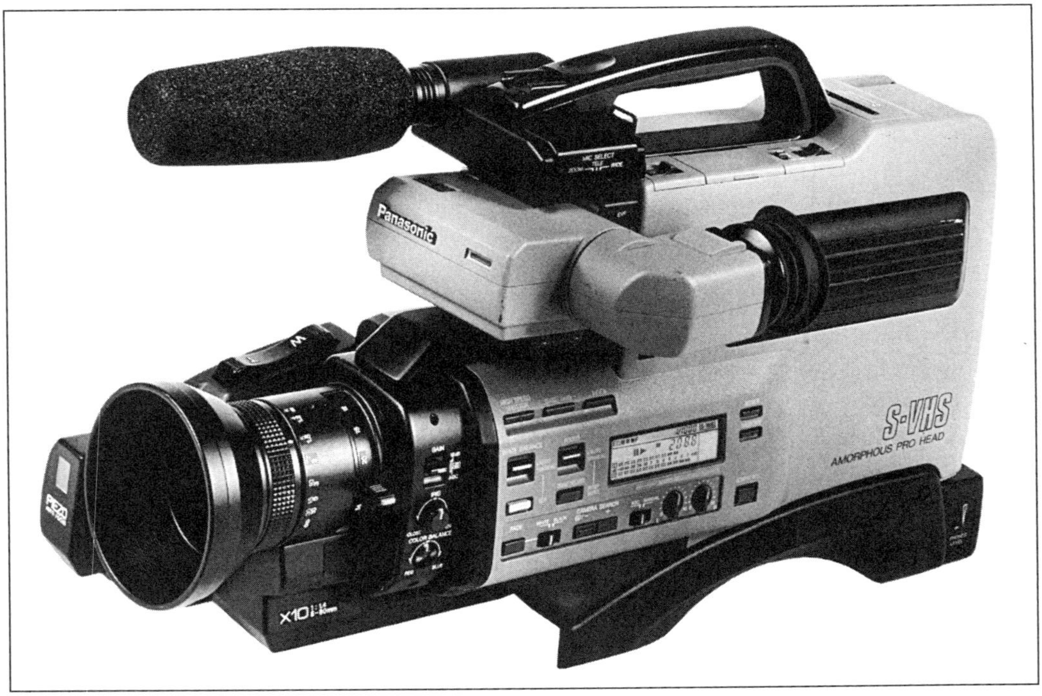

Super VHS or S-VHS. (Courtesy Panasonic)

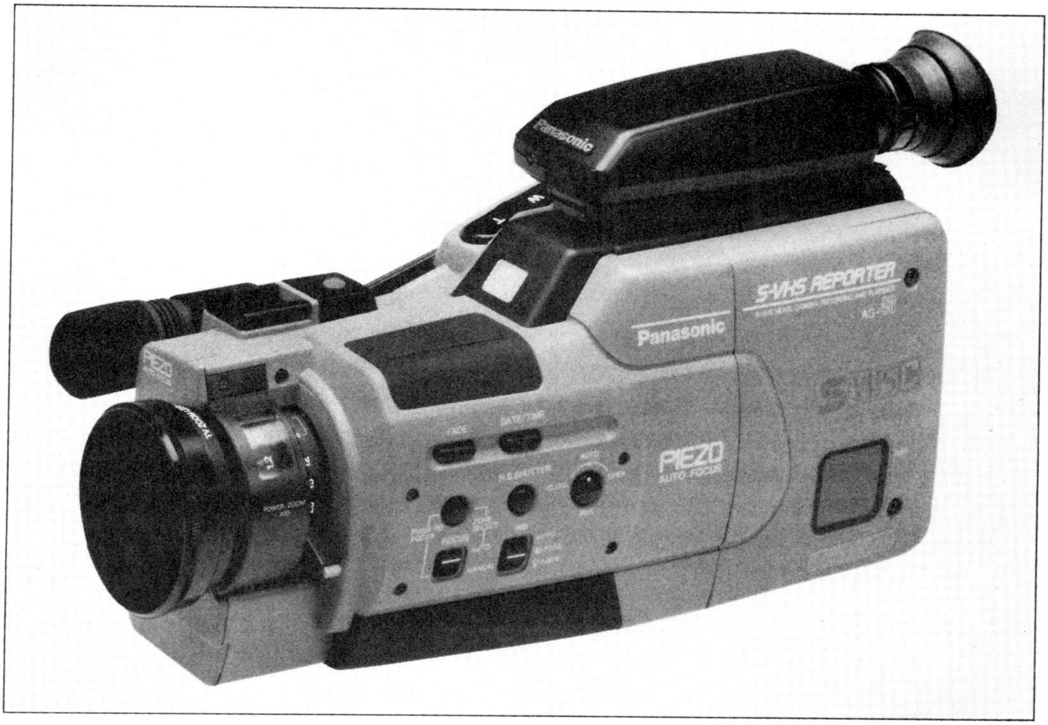

Compact super VHS or S-VHS-C. (Courtesy Panasonic)

The 8mm Family

The other major group of formats gets its name from the 8-millimeter-wide videotape used. This tape is metallic-particle-based, as compared with the plastic-oxide construction of VHS tape. The 8mm format yields high-resolution pictures, concert-hall sound, and superior reproduction qualities. The sound is superior to VHS because the audio is recorded across the tape, mixed with the video signal, rather than being confined to a narrow track as on VHS and S-VHS tapes. This means you can't audio-dub replacement sound over a portion of the original soundtrack as you can with VHS, but this isn't a major loss, since most editing of the soundtrack in any format occurs when you make a second-generation copy of the original tape (see Chapter 5). Some of Sony's top-of-the-line Hi-8 video cameras and VCRs have a PCM (Pulse Code Modulation) track, which does allow you to record a separate, secondary soundtrack on the original tape.

Another advantage of 8mm tapes is that they are smaller and play more slowly than VHS tapes; an 8mm tape plays 1 or 2 hours, versus 30 minutes or so for VHS-C and S-VHS-C tapes.

The drawback is that 8mm is not compatible with VHS, and if your home VCR is in the VHS format, you'll either have to go out and buy new equipment or connect the 8mm camera directly to the television to play back the recorded tapes. If you plan to do any editing, be aware that a second-generation copy dubbed from a VHS tape will show a small but noticeable loss of picture quality on your television monitor. A copy of an 8mm tape will probably have less loss. For duplication, the super, enhanced versions of both formats greatly alleviate this problem.

Like the VHS family, the 8mm family is divided into standard and super formats. The standard format is known simply as *8mm*; the super format is called *Hi-8*.

Standard 8mm

Of the 8mm formats, the standard 8mm (sometimes called Video 8) is easily the most popular. The picture quality equals or exceeds VHS, and the digital sound (both mono and stereo) is superior to that of VHS. Along with good sound and picture, 8mm brings the advantage of compact size both in cameras and tapes.

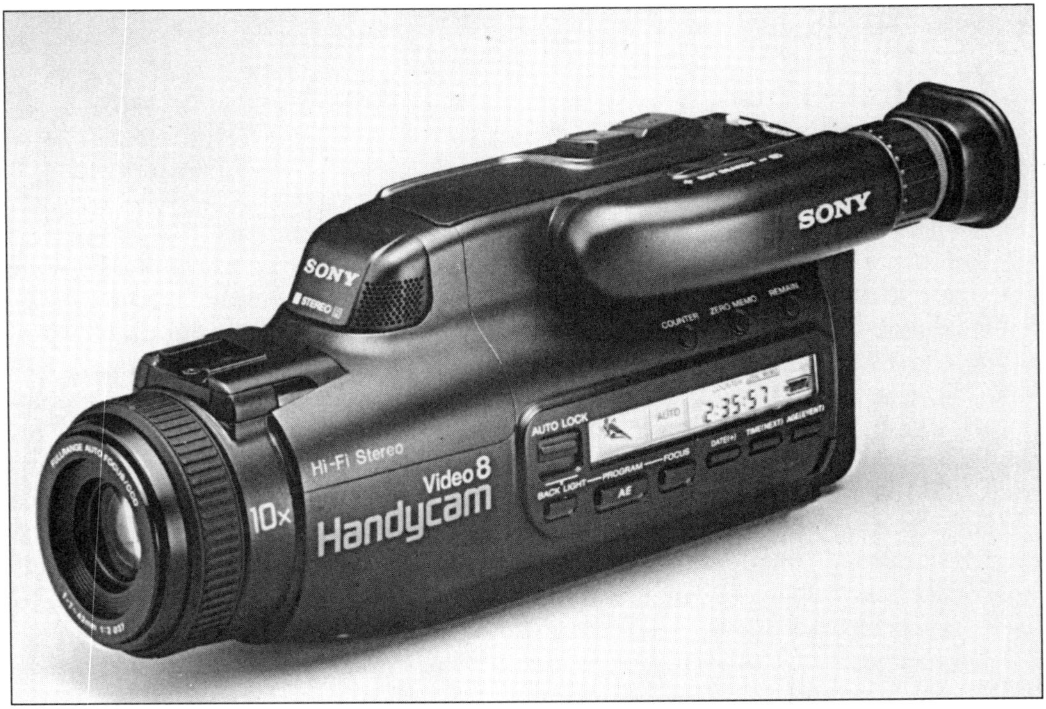

Standard 8mm or video 8. (Courtesy Sony)

Hi-8

Hi-8 (or high-band 8) is the super version of 8mm. The high-resolution tapes provide unsurpassed picture and sound quality, equal to S-VHS. Be aware, though, that although you can play standard 8mm tapes on Hi-8 equipment, you can't play Hi-8 tapes on standard 8mm equipment. The standard equipment simply can't handle the high-resolution tapes.

Palmcorders

Palmcorders don't represent a format of their own—indeed, there are both VHS and 8mm models available—but they're becoming so popular, they deserve some special attention. These cameras look like a dream come true: so small and lightweight (as little as 1.2 pounds, not including battery) that you can hold them in the palm of your hand. Unfortunately, that's both an advantage and a

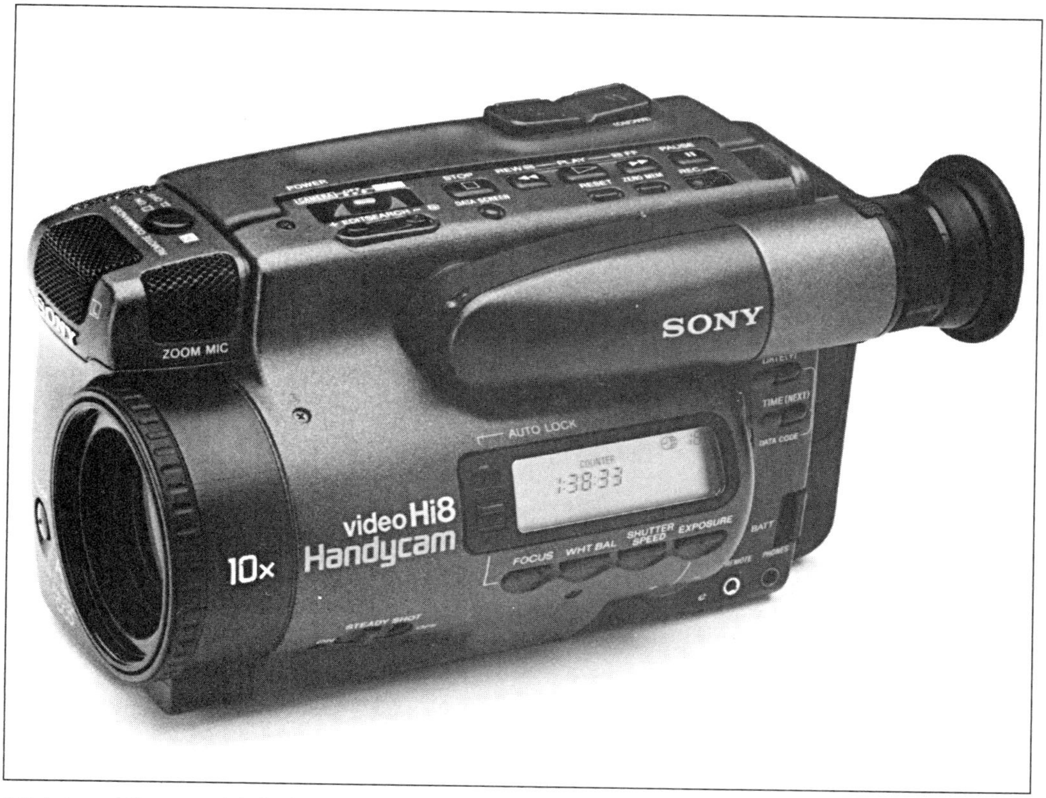

High-band 8mm or Hi-8. (Courtesy Sony)

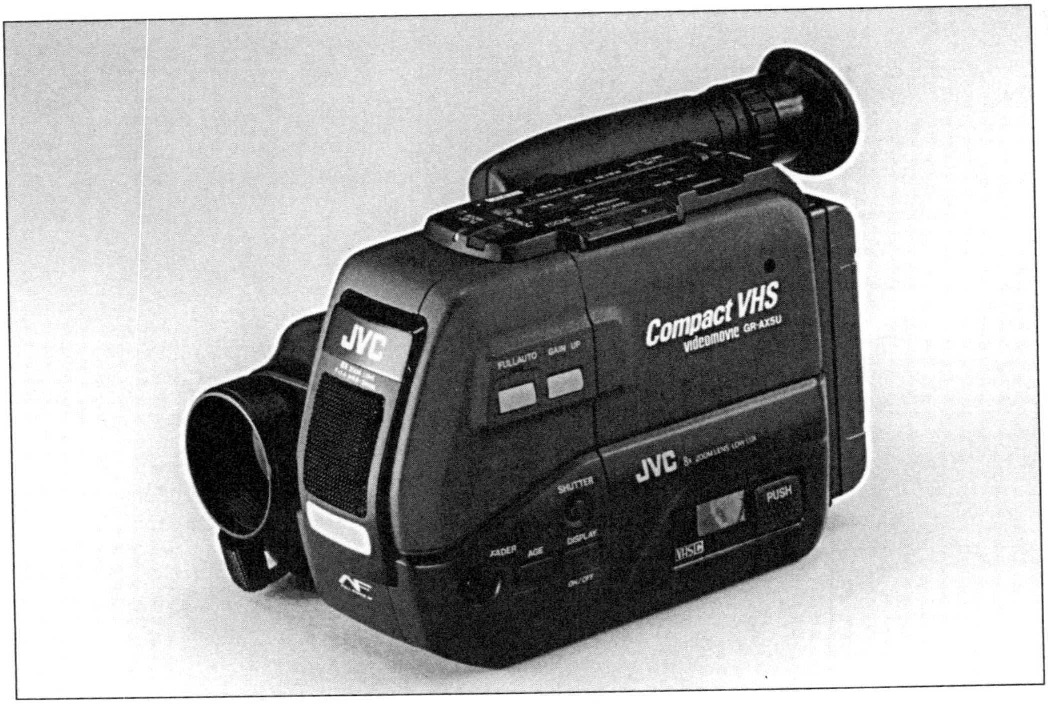

Palmcorder. (Courtesy JVC)

disadvantage. Since they're so small, you have nothing to brace them against; even the slightest jiggle of your hand or arm translates into shaky images on the screen, and it's most noticeable in close-up shots. This might not be a major issue to people who just use the camera for fun, but it could hinder the efforts of the videographer trying to produce more professional-looking results.

If you decide on a palmcorder, concentrate on bracing yourself when you shoot and keeping the camera level and steady. Hold your elbows close to your sides; if your arms flap about, the motion will certainly be transmitted to the image on the screen. Another tip for steadying yourself involves the viewfinder. Many palmcorders have a movable viewfinder that swings to an upright position to make low-level shots easier, but it can also be used to provide extra stability. Hold the camera close to your body about chest high, support it with both arms, and tilt the viewfinder to about 45 degrees. In 1992, Sony and Canon offered 8mm palmcorders that compensate automatically for a shaky hand with built-in motion compensators.

Some Advice for the First-Time Buyer

As technology improves, manufacturers seem to be making fewer full-size video cameras in favor of the smaller hand-held models. The few large cameras still on retailers' shelves could mean a bargain for the first-time buyer on a limited budget. If you already own a VCR in the VHS format and want to try shooting videos, shop around for a second-hand VHS camera or even a new basic model that's been passed up by compact- and feature-hungry buyers. You might just find that a full-size camera with simple, basic controls suits your needs when starting out. Aside from the sheer simplicity of operation of these models, the extra size and heft can be an advantage. A full-size camera is steady and reassuring to hold.

THE LENS

The value of a good *lens* can't be overstated. It must be capable of pulling in faint light and of shooting clear close-ups as well as telephoto scenes. Without a good lens, you simply won't get clear images. Fortunately, the standard lenses on almost all video cameras today rival the best optical devices available to film-camera professionals just a few years ago.

The measure of a good lens begins with its construction. Look for all-glass optics instead of plastic components. Although video cameras from the major companies have glass optics, it doesn't hurt to ask; some lower-priced models from lesser-known manufacturers might use plastic.

For outdoor videos, your camera's lens must be as versatile as possible: capable of close-ups as well as telephoto shots, and adaptable to many different light conditions. Here again, the standard lenses on most medium- to high-priced cameras meet these criteria. Things can quickly become confusing, though, when you compare cameras and lenses in the electronics supermarket.

The advertising brochures produced by video manufacturers often refer to their lenses as *zoom lenses* with a certain power ratio, perhaps 10-to-1 or 12-to-1. Zoom is a feature of modern optics that allows for variable *focal lengths* within one lens. The focal length of a lens is the distance behind the surface of the lens, measured in millimeters, that an incoming image appears in clear, precise focus. The different focal lengths of different lenses are a guide to their power and function.

In video, the focal length that comes closest to reproducing the image seen by the human eye is about 7mm to 10mm for palmcorders that use a ⅓-inch imaging chip (CCD), 10mm for the many cameras that use a ½-inch CCD, and 13mm for those older models using a ⅔-inch chip. Focal lengths shorter than these provide a more wide-angle view, and longer focal lengths provide a more telephoto view. It should be noted that no standard zoom lens for a video camera gives much wide-angle capability, which can be a source of frustration if your goal, for example, is a close-up shot of a large group of people. A wide-angle lens extender (see Chapter 2) will help. A few cameras have been manufactured with the ability to accept interchangeable lenses, just as a 35mm still camera can, but these are not yet widely marketed. Zoom lenses with focal lengths reaching 80mm to 100mm provide good telephoto capability for most of the scenes you'll shoot. A zoom lens with a 10-to-1 ratio

UNDERSTANDING ZOOM LENSES

A sales feature for video cameras and lenses is zoom power—that is, the range you can shoot from the wide-angle setting to the telephoto magnification. It's usually shown as 8x, 10x, or 12x. Eight-power (8x) magnification means the image at the wide-angle setting can be enlarged eight times when you use the maximum telephoto setting. Ten-power zoom (10x) enlarges your subject 10 times; 12x, 12 times.

Keep in mind that although the zoom power might be the same for two lenses, if the range of focal lengths (the optical dimensions) of the two lenses are different, the actual zoom range will also be different. The optical dimensions are printed on the side of every lens, and the numbers appear in the small print in the sales literature. Furthermore, the size of the camera's imaging chip (CCD) also affects the equation. It can be confusing, so read the small print to find out what kind of lens you're buying. For example, a catalog might list four cameras for sale: three have 8x power zoom lenses, and one has 12x zoom. How can you compare the zoom power on the cameras? Take a look at the following chart.

Camera	CCD Width	Zoom Power	Optical Dimensions
#1	½ inch	8	6.2–49.6mm
#2	⅓ inch	8	8.5–68mm
#3	½ inch	8	7–56mm
#4	½ inch	12	6.5–78mm

Of the first three cameras, all with 8x zooms, camera #2 has more telephoto power for distance shots (shown by the higher number in its range of optical dimensions *and* its smaller imaging chip). Indeed, because of the smaller chip size of camera #2, the maximum focal length for telephoto shots (68mm) is about the equivalent of 90mm for a camera with a ½-inch chip, and thus exceeds even camera #4. However, the 8.5mm setting at the lower end of the range for camera #2 means less wide-angle capability than is available on the other cameras. Camera #4, with the 12x zoom, has practically the same wide-angle capability as camera #1 (6.5mm as opposed to 6.2mm), but has more telephoto magnification (78mm) than cameras #1 or #3.

(called a 10-power zoom) might have focal lengths ranging from 8mm to 80mm, which means that the image you see in the viewfinder at the 8mm setting will appear 10 times larger at the 80mm setting.

The development of the zoom lens for video cameras means that one lens can do the work of three or four fixed-focal-length lenses, plus all the ranges in between. To a professional photographer, the zoom lens is a compromise: it's convenient, but the optical quality suffers somewhat when compared with separate fixed-focal-length

APERTURE CONTROL: ALL ABOUT F-STOPS

The *iris diaphragm* of an adjustable lens has many possible settings from wide open to tightly closed. Wide open, it lets in more light than when it's closed. With automatic aperture control, an infinite number of settings vary the amount of light coming in through the lens. The camera circuitry senses the amount of light in the scene and automatically adjusts the aperture. With manual control, there are numerous predetermined settings (positions of the iris) called *f-stops* and written as *f/*. If you use manual aperture control, you must select the correct f-stop for the illumination of your scene. The standard f-stops are firmly established in photography. These are relative values, and are expressed as follows: f/1, f/1.4, f/2, f/3.5, f/4, f/5.6, f/8, f/11, f/16, f/32, f/45, and f/64. That is the full range of f-stops, but most cameras, especially video cameras, have a more limited range. Some combination of these numbers will appear on your video camera lens as aperture settings for manual control.

The lowest f-stop corresponds to the aperture at its most open position. It also signifies the focal ratio of the lens. For example, a lens with a focal ratio of 1:1.4 has a maximum aperture setting of 1.4, and the f-stop at this position is f/1.4. Photographers use the maximum aperture setting to identify a lens in terms of its light-gathering ability. This is known as the relative *speed* of a lens. A fast lens gathers more light than does a slow lens because it has a wider initial aperture setting. An f/1.4 lens is a very fast lens, faster than an f/2 lens. As the numbers increase, the opening gets smaller and less light is allowed to pass. F/16 is a very small aperture.

lenses. Zoom lenses are only marginally inferior, however, and should not concern the amateur videographer planning to shoot a wide variety of subjects.

Zoom lenses are standard equipment on video cameras. They're both good and especially convenient for the average user. Since zoom lenses vary in power, check the specifications carefully before buying your first video camera. The zooms offer every combination from wide angle to telephoto in one package, but the sales brochures habitually refer to these qualities in general terms like, "Big, 10-power zoom lets you shoot close-up or far away!" This is not helpful.

What is helpful is the range of focal lengths (the optical dimensions) printed on the side of every zoom lens. In these ranges, the lower number refers to the wide-angle capability, and the higher number refers to the telephoto capability. For example, one zoom lens might have a range from 8mm (wide-angle capability) to 80mm (telephoto capability). This is a 10-power zoom with a reasonable wide-angle setting and fairly good telephoto reach. Another lens might also have a 10-power zoom, but the focal-length range might be from 10mm to 100mm. This is less of a wide-angle lens, but it has greater telephoto power. A 12x zoom, which might seem even more

DEPTH OF FIELD

Depth of field is a widely used term in photography that refers to how much of a picture appears in focus. We speak of a particular scene as having great depth of field when objects throughout the picture appear sharply in focus. There is limited depth of field when only the main subject is in focus and objects in front and behind are out of focus. The range of sharp focus provided by any fixed lens on a still camera is governed by the size of the aperture and the speed of the shutter. Since both aperture and shutter speed control the amount of light passing through the lens to form a recordable image, a balance must be struck between the two. You must first have enough light to see the subject. If the aperture is wide open, only the subject you focus on will be sharply defined; other objects will appear out of focus. If you close the aperture and reduce the shutter speed, more of the picture will be in focus—the depth of field will be greater.

With a zoom lens on a video camera, it's a little different. Shutter speed is not something you often vary, and aperture control is normally automatic (indeed, many cameras do not provide manual aperture control). Under these circumstances, by default, depth of field decreases with increasing focal length of the zoom, and increases with the distance to the object in principal focus.

When you use automatic aperture control, the camera sets the aperture for the available light. Unless your subject is backlighted or highlighted, the exposure will be correct, and the depth of field will be the greatest possible under those automatically controlled conditions. Look at the picture in the viewfinder and determine just how much you want to be in focus.

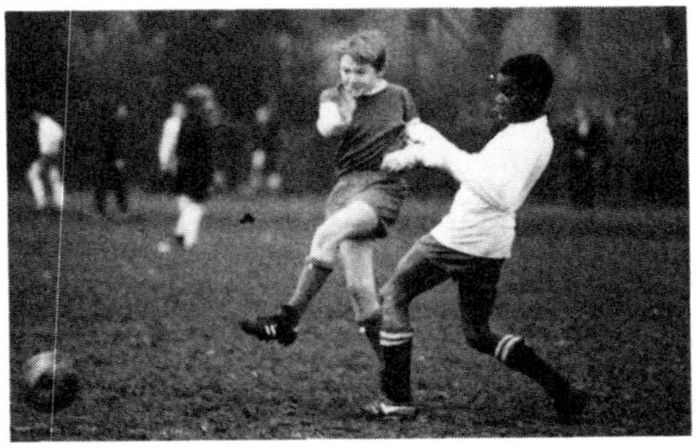

Shallow depth of field is illustrated here. The emphasis is on the players and the background is blurred.

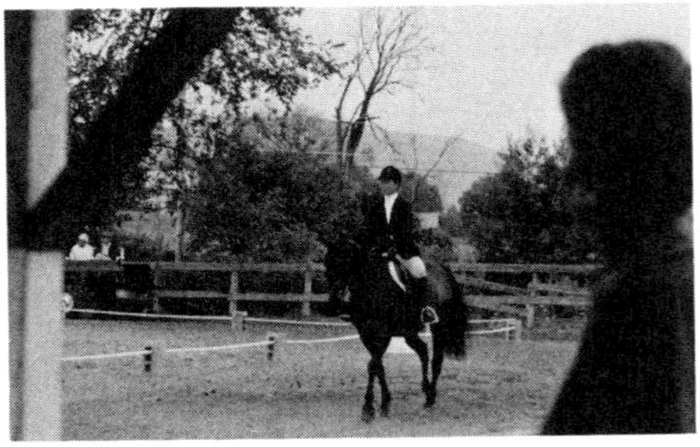

Here there is equal emphasis on the setting, rider, and horse, and only the spectator in the foreground is blurred.

powerful, could begin at 8mm (only slightly more wide angle) and go up to 96mm (fractionally less at the telephoto end).

Here's one place where video and still cameras differ. Putting a 100mm lens on a 35mm still camera magnifies the image only about 3 times; using the 100mm

SHUTTER SPEED: SHOOTING FAST ACTION

Good film cameras have more than a dozen shutter speeds from which to choose, ranging from a fixed open position all the way to something as quick as 1/4,000 of a second. The standard speed for video is 1/60 of a second, which is the speed at which the charge-coupled device (CCD) processes images (frames) and transmits them as electrical signals to the tape, and is also roughly the speed at which the human eye perceives action. Viewing the action recorded at this speed will look very much the way you see things in real life. For very fast action, however, you might want to use a faster speed. Adjustable speeds of 1/10,000 of a second or faster produce sharp, clear pictures for your action video, eliminating even the blur of the swing of a baseball bat or a golf club. But there is a caveat: Since the CCD continues to process images at 60 frames per second, faster speeds leave freeze-frame gaps in the recording, almost like a strobe light. The effect might be barely noticeable at a speed of, say, 1/250 of a second. If fast-action sports videos are your particular interest, this will be a fertile area for experimentation.

If you increase the shutter speed, you must compensate for less light passing through the lens by opening the aperture. If you widen the aperture, though, you'll get less depth of field, so careful focusing becomes even more important. Check the image in the viewfinder until you see the results you want.

setting on a video camera, however, magnifies the image 10 to 15 times. So whereas a 100mm lens has only limited telephoto capability on a still camera, it has good telephoto capability on a video camera.

Many zoom lenses also have a macro position that enables you to shoot just 4 inches or less (for some lenses, less than 1 cm) from your subject. Spectacular close-up scenes of flowers or butterflies are routine with the macro setting. It's outside the range of the regular zoom controls on the lens, and is usually set by a manual adjustment to the lens itself. It's not a feature you'll use frequently, but it's nice to have as standard equipment. It provides more flexibility to your video shooting plans.

Another factor to consider in a lens is its light-gathering capability. An indication of quality in a lens and good light-gathering ability is a small focal ratio, such as 1:1.4 (often called a 1.4 lens or an f/1.4 lens). Higher numbers, such as 1:3.5 or 1:4, indicate less light-gathering ability. These numbers are printed on the side of every lens, so don't believe it when the salesperson boasts, "This little beauty has a really fast lens for close-up action and faraway zooms to pull in the wing flutter of an eagle. It's got an f/4 lens!"

This number also identifies the lens in terms of its widest possible *aperture* opening. The smaller the number, the wider the aperture opening, and the more light it can gather. Later in this chapter we'll look at manual aperture controls and lens settings.

FEATURES AND CONTROLS

All video cameras today have automatic controls for focusing, aperture, and shutter speeds. They're all handled by the computer circuitry inside the camera. All have automatic zoom lenses to give you wide-angle to telephoto shots at the push of a button. The automatic zoom, which provides a smooth transition from one focal length to another without interruption, is controlled by a toggle switch, often labeled with a T for telephoto on one side and a W for wide-angle on the other side.

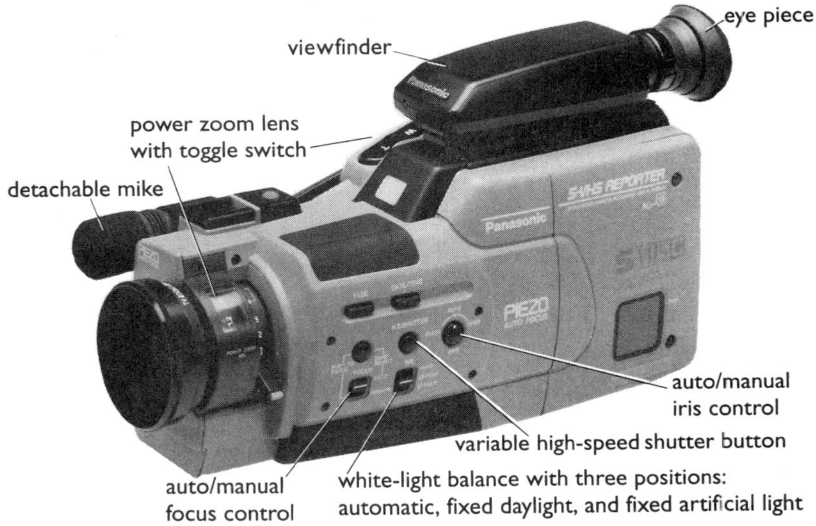

Power Zoom Lens with Toggle Switch: *An all-in-one lens, standard on most video cameras, that is capable of wide-angle to zoom shots. Lens power varies from model to model. The toggle switch enables you to adjust the focal length while you shoot.* ***Auto/Manual Focus:*** *When set on automatic, most video cameras unfortunately will focus on the nearest large object near the center of the screen, possibly altering focal distance and the depth of field in ways you did not intend: as your subject moves off into the distance, the automatic sensors might focus on a tree in the foreground. By switching to manual, you can selectively focus on the subject even as it moves away or to the left or right.* ***White-Light Balance:*** *Corrects ambient light to produce properly balanced, neutral light, which ensures that all other colors appear natural. Some cameras enable you to adjust white-light balance manually, a big advantage in conditions that can fool the automatic mode.* ***Variable High-Speed Shutter:*** *Increases shutter speed, enabling you to capture fast-action outdoor scenes.* ***Auto/Manual Iris:*** *Enables a switch to manual iris (or aperture) control whenever the automatic sensors are likely to be fooled by contrasting light conditions. (Courtesy Panasonic)*

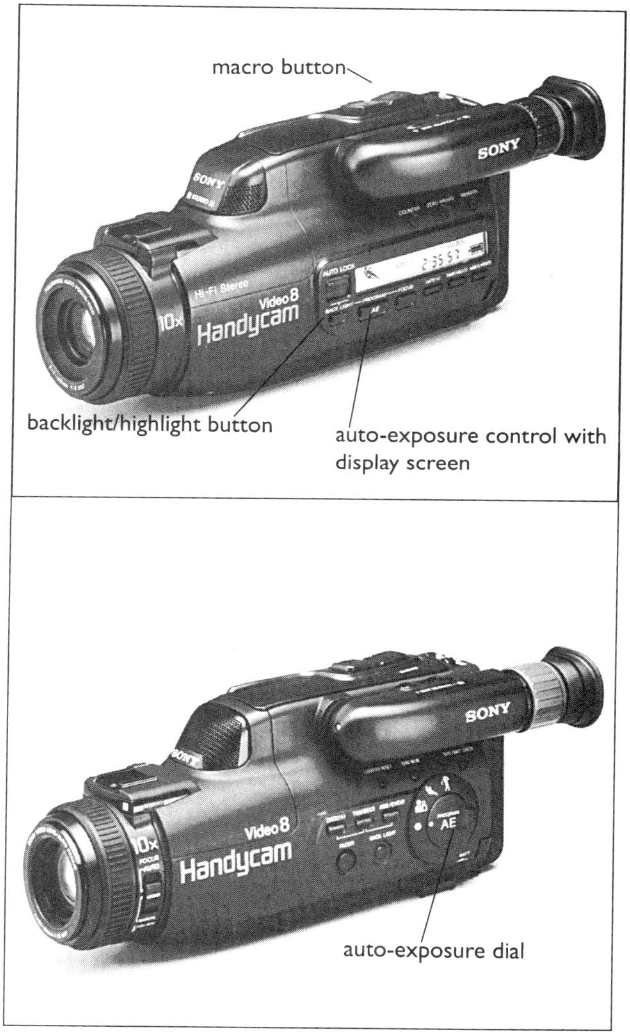

Auto Exposure: *This feature of some Sony cameras offers various options for setting focus and aperture. You can combine automatic aperture settings with manual shutter speed selections, or adjust aperture manually, or pick one of two or three automatic setting combinations for "portrait shots" or shooting fast action.* ***Macro:*** *A zoom-lens feature that enables you to shoot only a few inches from the subject—or even a fraction of an inch—to create spectacular close-ups.* ***Backlight/Highlight:*** *The backlight feature overlooks bright background light and exposes for the subject. Highlight compensates for areas of unusually high contrast. (Courtesy Sony)*

When you look at a camera in the store, check its automatic focus and zoom capabilities. Using the viewfinder, pick out a nearby subject and then one farther away (in auto-focus mode the camera focuses on the largest object in view near the center of the frame). Does the camera stay focused when you shift from one object to the other? It should. It should also hold focus when you toggle the automatic zoom switch from wide-angle to telephoto or vice-versa. A few cameras have a tracking feature so that even if the subject moves from "center stage," it will remain in focus.

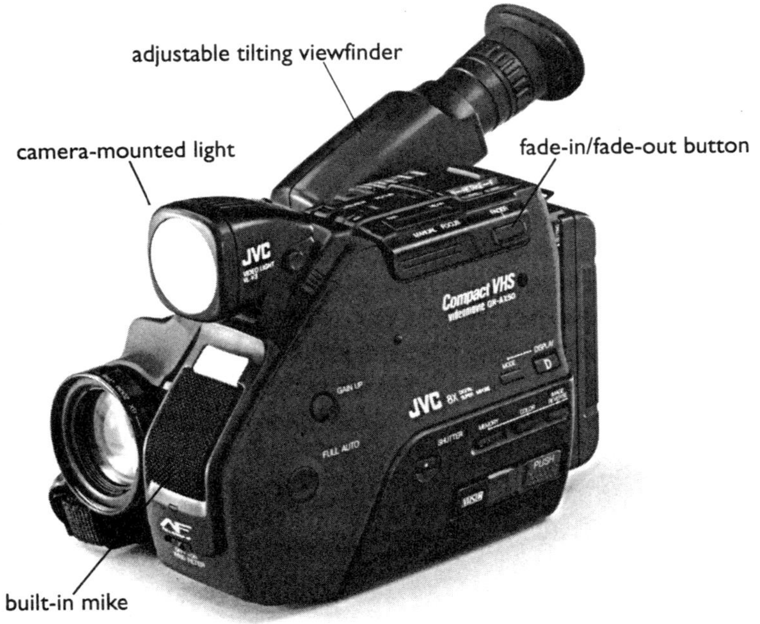

Camera-mounted Light: *Despite the limitations of camera-mounted lights—most project a harsh, flat light that is good for only short distances and creates a spotlight effect—they're better than no light. This feature can provide fill-in light when the sun is behind the subject or when ambient light is insufficient.* ***Built-in Mike:*** *Whether stereo or mono, these mikes may pick up internal camera noise. The more common external mikes are better in this regard, but still limited by the fact that they're mounted on the camera, not on the subject being videotaped. It's best to look for a camera that has a jack for attaching a remote mike—a real plus for outdoor videography.* ***Fade-in/Fade-out:*** *An in-camera editing feature that enables you to dissolve from one scene to another. This feature is more useful on your editing equipment than on the camera. Remember: Once you've added this effect to a scene, you can't remove it without cutting the scene altogether. (Courtesy JVC)*

A versatile camera should also have a few manual controls that enable you to select not only what you shoot, but how. Possibilities are manual focus, manual zoom, manual aperture setting, variable shutter speed, a switch for backlighting and highlighting, white-light balance, and a start/stop switch. Additional features are like icing on a cake: nice for special occasions, but adding considerably to the cost.

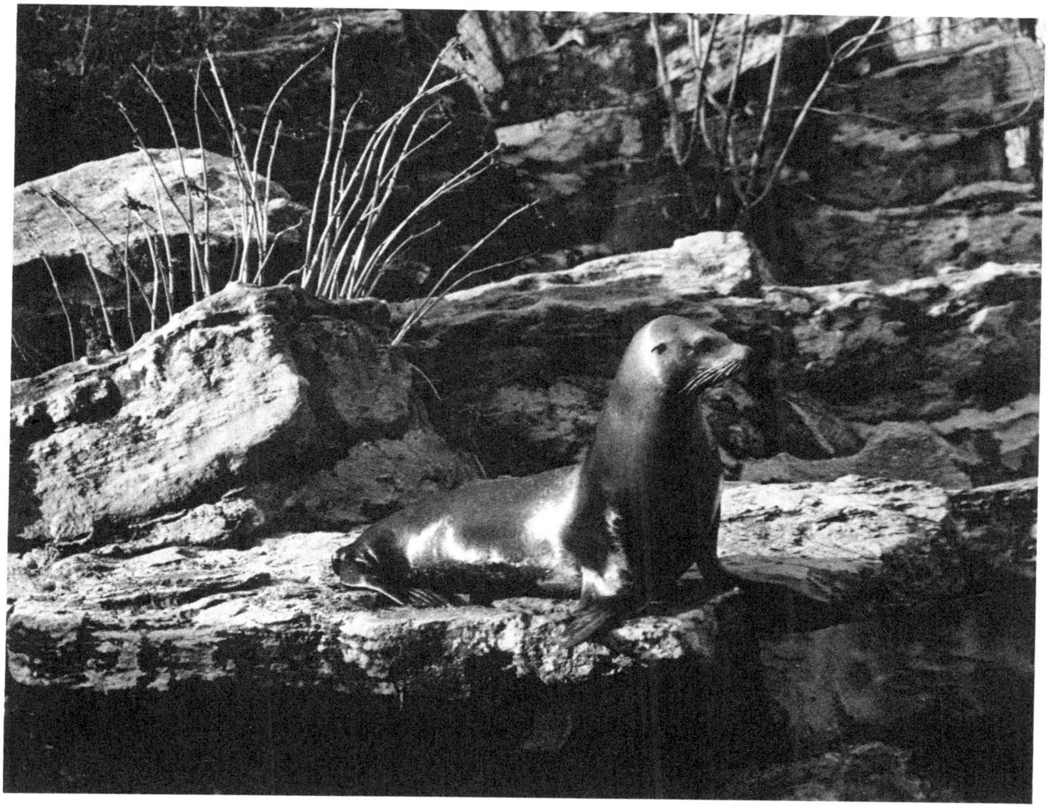

Both the subject and the background have contrasting light and dark spots, and glare—from the sleek body of the sea lion and from the sunlight reflecting off the wet rocks. Automatic settings will work best, allowing the light sensors in the camera to balance these elements electronically for an evenly lighted picture. As the sea lion dives into the pool, follow the action. The automatic sensors will quickly compensate for the darker expanse of water and open the aperture to let in more light.

Manual Focus

With automatic focusing, the camera's sensors focus on the nearest large object in the middle of the viewing area. The camera makes the decision, not you. This could mean a tree or a fence in the foreground is in sharp focus, while your subject, people walking down a country lane, is not. Whenever there is a large group of moving objects, the lens automatically adjusts every time one object or another moves toward the center of view, detracting from the broad scene you want to shoot. A

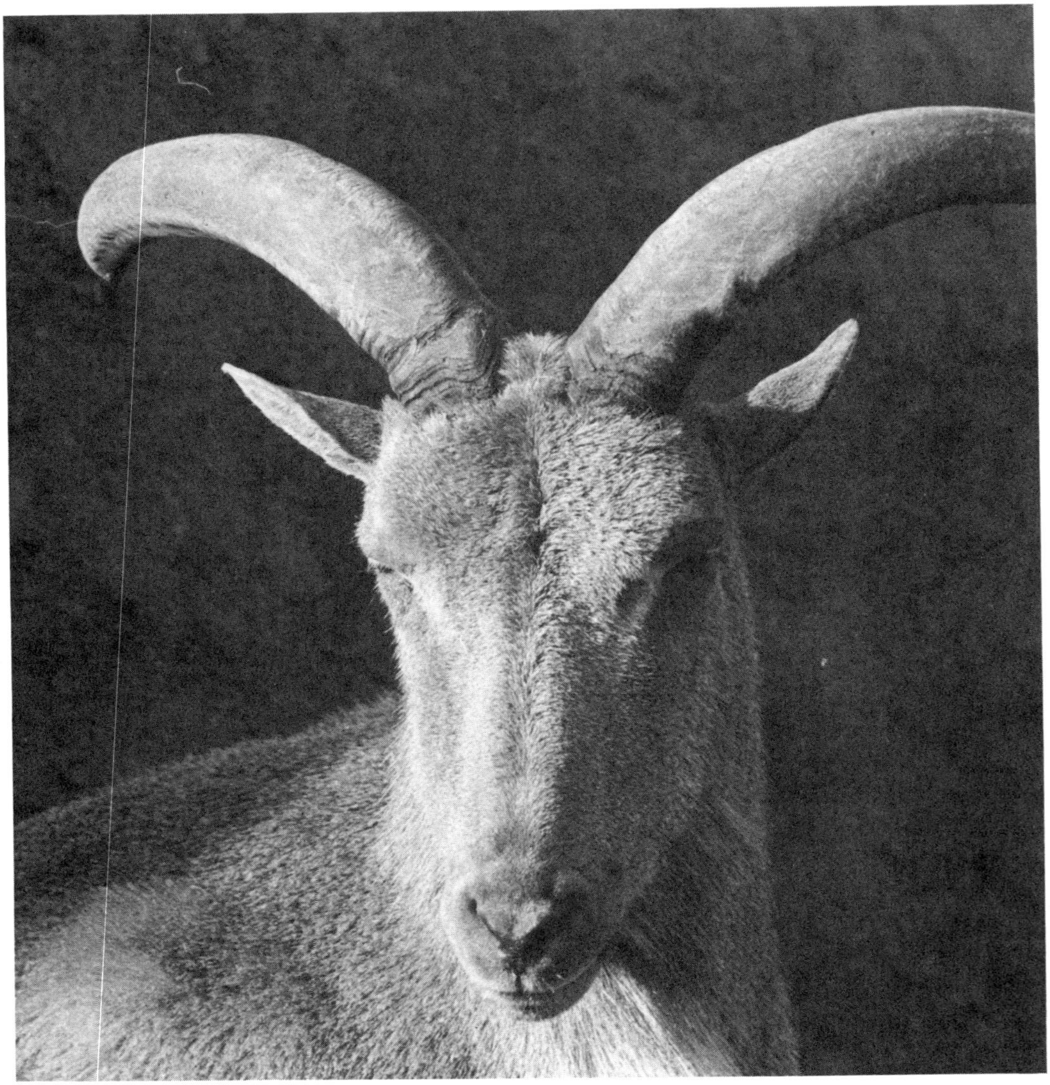

Tight focusing on the subject with the background obscured. The auto-focus setting might capture this shot, but any movement of the goat would activate the sensors, causing the focus to shift. Manual focusing is better here. If the animal moves, you can follow it without changing focus and without bringing the background into prominence. Another consideration in outdoor scenes is the natural light falling on the subject. Here the light source (the sun) is behind the videographer's left shoulder, producing good highlights on the goat and bringing life to an otherwise flat picture. An automatic iris (or aperture) control could be fooled by a dark background and cttempt to balance the total light—with detrimental results.

better choice would be to override the automatic focus with selective manual focusing, which lets you choose a specific distance for the point of focus. From an artistic perspective, manual focusing can be a very creative tool. You might choose to keep the foreground images out of focus and have your subject in the background in sharp, clear focus.

Manual Zoom

Most of the time, you'll shoot your videos with full automatic zoom, but there might be times when you want specific control to pre-set the focal length of your lens to a certain distance, or even to do a partial zoom by hand. The automatic zoom is controlled by a motor that moves the zoom at a certain speed, which might not suit your needs. At a baseball game you might be using a wide-angle setting to take in the whole field when the batter hits the ball. When the throw comes to the plate, though, you'll have to zoom in fast to get the play. The automatic zoom might not be fast enough to catch the action, so you'll have to zoom manually. Good cameras permit this, and also have an override button that instantly restores the power zoom.

Manual Aperture

Some video cameras come with built-in automatic aperture, or iris, control. Like the iris in your eye, the aperture of the camera lens opens and closes to let in the proper amount of light for the existing conditions. But unlike your eye, the camera can be fooled by some light conditions, resulting in a bad picture with distorted lighting. The most common example of this is a brightly illuminated background scene contrasted by a darker subject in the foreground.

Picture a beach under the noonday sun. Your subject is a small cluster of kids playing at the water's edge. The camera's light sensors reflect a bright picture overall, and the automatic aperture closes to let in less light. Unfortunately, this robs your subject of the necessary light for proper illumination, so the kids appear too dark on your viewing screen. In photography, you would say the subject is underexposed. To compensate for this, you need to open the aperture manually to give proper exposure to the subject, allowing for a little overexposure (too much light) of the background. The nice thing about video is that you can see the effects for yourself in the viewfinder before you shoot. This manual iris adjustment alters the parameters of the camera's automatic exposure system, so the camera will continue to overexpose until you make the counteracting manual adjustment.

The other common use of manual iris control is to fade in or fade out a scene, by opening the iris from its fully closed position or by gradually closing it to black. Some cameras that lack manual iris control do have a fade button.

Variable Shutter Speed

Somewhat related to aperture settings is variable shutter speed, an added feature on some video cameras. A faster shutter speed option is likely to prove helpful for capturing outdoor action.

Backlighting and Highlighting

Most cameras have a switch offering two alternative aperture settings: One setting corrects for simple backlighted conditions, and the other corrects for highlighted conditions. In a backlighted situation, the light source is behind the subject and the subject is in relative darkness. In effect, the backlight setting directs the camera to overlook the bright background light and expose for the subject.

In highlighted situations, a single but intense light source creates one or more areas of unusually high contrast. It's a relatively dark scene overall, so the automatic aperture opens to let in more light. But the subject in the spotlight is overexposed and might be washed out. To compensate for this, use the highlight switch.

This backlighting/highlighting capability doesn't give you the range of control over f-stops that you get with a manual iris adjustment, but it's enough for most users and most situations. Put another way, it's the minimum degree of aperture control you should accept when you shop for a video camera.

White-Light Balance

Visible light is actually made up of many colors, but the human brain blends these colors to produce an even, neutral light we call *white light*. But the quality of white light differs with venue—outdoors versus indoors, incandescent versus fluorescent lighting. Sunlight is "hotter," indoor lighting, "cooler." The human eye unconsciously adjusts for these differences, but the camera's eye has a hard time doing so. Thus, a white-light balance correction is absolutely necessary in all video work to make the camera record and reproduce properly balanced, natural-looking light. Most of the time, your camera does this automatically, but under some conditions, the automatic correction will not work effectively. The camera should have a manual white-balance switch to set the standard for "white" for the camera in prevailing conditions, thus ensuring that all other colors appear natural. Correcting the white balance manually varies from camera to camera, so check your owner's manual for the proper method.

Start/Stop Switch

In addition to the power switch that turns the camera on and off, good video cameras have a start/stop switch that keeps the camera unit in a standby mode: warmed up and ready to go, but with certain functions (such as automatic focus and aperture) in a resting mode. This cuts down substantially on battery use, and is useful when your shooting is interrupted for a short period, but you still want to be ready when the action resumes. Without this feature, each time you wanted to resume shooting, you'd have to turn on the camera, reset the white-light balance, and adjust the focus and other functions. The start/stop switch bypasses this bothersome and time-consuming process.

ATTACHED VCR

Almost every full-size amateur video camera manufactured today has a VCR built in and directly connected to the video camera. It's such an obvious addition, it's surprising to know that as late as 1984, books on the subject of home video production mentioned the *possibility* of integrating the separate VCR with the camera. This, of course, would be in the future, as the technology improved. Well, the future is now, and the integrated VCR is not only a reality, it's basic.

The VCR in your camera is essentially the same as the larger unit you probably have at home connected to your TV, but with limited extra features. Your camera VCR has the same *tape transport system* (the recording and playback heads) as your home unit, and can be used as a primary videotape source when playing back a tape or even editing. Its first function, however, is to record and play back the scenes you shoot. It gives you instant review of the material shot.

You'll see the term *flying erase heads* on almost all video cameras. Insist on them. They originated with Sony engineers, but they've spread to many other manufacturers. This feature facilitates smooth recording and editing by positioning the record, playback, and erase heads close to each other and in the same plane. The result is start and stop operations that are smooth and free from the annoying flashes of light and bars of static called *glitches* that appear at the end of scenes recorded on earlier models. This means much less work later on if you decide to do serious editing.

Most video cameras have a *preview switch* that enables you to backtrack the videotape to see what came immediately before you stopped taping. Look for this feature when you buy a video camera.

While you're considering the playback capabilities of the video camera, give some thought to the viewfinder. I mentioned earlier that the viewfinder is actually a miniature TV screen. Today the electronic circuitry is governed by charge-coupled devices (CCDs) that link up with integrated printed circuits. It's enough to know that your camera and viewfinder should be of solid-state CCD construction. In all likelihood, anything less is probably not even available any longer.

The VCR unit should also have all the normal VCR controls, such as forward, fast forward, reverse or rewind, and stop. These are usually identified by little arrowheads stamped on the switches. An on-off power switch, tape cartridge eject button, connections for earphones and remote-control devices, and a counter-reset switch complete the basic controls for the camera-attached VCR. One additional control that is very useful when editing is the *pause switch* to stop and hold a single picture or to use when editing with the camera.

The VCR unit should have a separate recording switch so you can use it as a backup to or instead of your home VCR. In addition, there should be a switch that electronically isolates the playback tape from other controls in the VCR and permits you to make a direct connection via cable to another VCR for editing. (You'll learn about editing in Chapter 5.) This switch bypasses the normal playback viewing circuits, thereby transferring the audio and video quality on the original tape to the tape in the second VCR with minimal loss of signal. Many other features, including cross-fade, fade-out, and character generators (which enable you to print captions or titles) are wonderful to have, and might even be included as standard features on top-of-the-line video cameras, but they're much more useful as features on the special editing equipment you'll use later on. Whether you include them on the camera unit depends on how much you want to spend.

INPUT/OUTPUT CONNECTIONS

Every video camera needs a pair of connectors, called *jacks*, to facilitate the transfer of audio and video signals from the camera to a separate editing or playback VCR. These are the *signal output jacks.* Similarly, a good camera with a VCR should have a second pair of jacks built in for inputting audio and visual signals. A separate plug or jack for an external microphone is essential for outdoor videos in which remote sound recording is necessary or desirable.

SOUND RECORDING

All video cameras have a built-in microphone as part of the standard package. It's mounted on the camera body as far forward as possible to pick up sound from the subject in front of the lens. Microphones record either mono or stereo sound. Stereo is better, but it's more expensive, and the benefit is lost unless every component in the recording/playback chain is stereophonic. Controls on some cameras can vary the sensitivity of the microphone to compensate for unwanted sound, such as wind noise. Another feature to look for, as mentioned above, is a separate external microphone jack for multiple sound recordings.

POWER SOURCE

The video camera must be powered by something, and outdoors that something is batteries. The standard power units are rechargeable nickel-cadmium batteries commonly called *nicads.* They're good, reliable, and expensive. Nicads usually last about two hours, more or less, so it pays to carry at least one spare; two are better. You might also want to get a recharger with AC and DC capabilities so that you can recharge your batteries either at home or from a boat or car with a 12-volt DC power supply and plug-in adapter.

Nicads have improved dramatically in recent years. Whereas once they developed a "memory" that affected their ability to store a full charge, this is no longer a problem. The only thing to remember is not to discharge a battery fully before recharging it, since doing so reduces battery life. Charge them periodically, even when you're not using them. Also, wait for the battery to cool down before recharging it; warm batteries won't recharge fully.

SOME TECHNICAL CONSIDERATIONS

There are a couple of other things worth considering when choosing video cameras. They're somewhat technical, but armed with just the simplest of definitions, you should be able to handle the jargon of the manufacturers' brochures. The charge-coupled devices (CCDs) I mentioned earlier gather the light from the subject and break it down into a vast number of picture elements, called *pixels.* The more pixels in your video system, the better it is. Most of the CCDs in use in today's video cameras yield 350,000 or more pixels, but that doesn't mean the rest of the camera's recording and playback electronics maintain that standard. A VHS camera with a 400,000-pixel CCD will not record or play back with the same resolution as an S-VHS camera with a similar CCD.

Another term in common use is *lux*, a measure of illumination. It's used to indicate how much light your camera requires to operate. Lux has all but replaced candle power as a measure of illumination. One lux is equal to 0.09 footcandles. One footcandle is the amount of light visible from one candle at a distance of one foot.

Advertising brochures note two figures for lux: a maximum illumination and a minimum illumination. The minimum figure is the more important because it reveals how little light is needed by your camera to record a scene. A top-of-the-line video camera can operate with less than 2 lux illumination, which is about one-fifth footcandle, or very little light indeed. Will you be shooting outdoor videos after sundown, by moonlight, or at dusk in deep shadows? Your ability to shoot scenes successfully under these conditions has improved dramatically because modern video cameras have working ranges far beyond those of old-fashioned movie film. They're good in virtually all light conditions from near darkness to the brilliant sunlight seen in the tropics or reflected off high mountain snow. The maximum illumination should be in excess of 100,000 lux to shoot under clear, brilliant conditions with full-color, accurate results.

A third consideration is *lines of horizontal resolution*, which is a technical measure for the quality of a television picture. Commercial television broadcasts are rated at approximately 600 lines of resolution, while amateur equipment is much lower, about 400 lines. It all has to do with electronically charged particles of light that form as tiny dots of color on the television screen. The number of dots in a line and the number of lines running vertically and horizontally across the screen form the basis for this measure. The important fact to remember is that amateur video equipment has less resolution, less quality, than does commercial television equipment, but it's improving. You can approach professional standards with good amateur electronics.

ALL ABOUT VIDEOTAPES

Throughout the year, promotionally minded manufacturers and distributors stage demonstrations of their products at major electronics stores. The retailers like the promotions because they generate sales; the company representatives get a chance to push their new lines of equipment; and the buying public has a good opportunity to see and use new equipment and to learn some production techniques from the professionals. Ask the manager of your favorite video equipment store if a special demonstration evening can be arranged in your area. They can be instructive as well as entertaining.

At one Sony demonstration hosted in my town, the company spokesman offered some worthwhile advice to prospective customers who were pricing and comparing videotapes. "Beware of manufacturers' claims of 'high-quality' and 'high-grade' tape," he said. "It means very little." This brought a wave of laughter from the audience, because as he spoke, we were holding new Sony VHS tape cassettes boldly marked "Extra Superior High-Grade Videotape for State-of-the-Art Performance." He had to backtrack a little to explain that while "high quality" was a nebulous term, Sony did give information about *signal-to-noise ratio*, which is a good indication of the quality of any tape. The signal-to-noise ratio determines whether the picture retains all its clarity and vividness—not only when first recorded, but also when being duplicated.

Signal-to-Noise Ratio

This business of noise is a little confusing, so here's a brief explanation of what it means and how it affects you. In the world of video, noise is not necessarily something you hear; it's more like electronic dirt—something that interferes with the clear signal being received by your video camera. *Audio noise* is usually described as a background hiss or hum that underscores the desired soundtrack you're recording. *Video noise* (often called glitches) usually manifests itself in the form of interference in the picture being recorded. Video noise can look like a series of wavering lines across the picture, or perhaps a quick, visible scratchiness in the scene.

The signal-to-noise ratio (SNR) is a comparison figure drawn from dividing the value of the signal (the desired audio or video material) by the value of the noise (the extraneous, unwanted material). The resultant figure, measured in decibels (dB), is the ratio of good signal to bad noise—hence, signal-to-noise ratio.

Noise is usually measured at a very low level, but any level at all interferes with the signal. Although no one has established exact figures for the desired signal-to-noise ratio, the consensus is that the higher the figure, the better the system. In other words, you're striving for more signal than noise. When comparing various systems from different manufacturers, look for the system with the highest signal-to-noise ratio.

Length of Play and Speed

Another feature to consider when choosing videotape is length of play. Longer playing times require longer tapes. But since these longer tapes must still fit in a standard cartridge, they must be thinner than regular tapes. Thinner tape is not as strong as thicker tape; it might stretch or break when used repeatedly.

Related to length of play is the speed of the tape as it passes over the recording heads. Faster speeds result in higher quality with better pictures and more precise definition. Slower speeds mean you use less tape, but you sacrifice some quality for quantity.

The best practical advice I can offer on the subject of buying videotape is to let your budget make the final determination. Buy a couple of tapes in your price range and try them out. Choose the one giving the best results and stick with it until you have the urge to make another comparison test against something new. Tapes will always vary in quality. Use what pleases you.

Durability

Here's a final note on the nature of videotape. This business is so new, no one knows how videotape will hold up over the years. It's generally acknowledged that videotape can be expected to lose some of its picture quality in about 10 years. On the plus side, videotape is easily duplicated and the dubbing process gets easier every year. To be on the safe side, make electronically enhanced copies of your important videotapes every 8 to 10 years. This is best done with two similar VCRs and the aid of a video processor (see Chapter 5), which can boost the video signal, minimize noise, and correct for any color loss.

CHAPTER TWO

Supplementary Equipment and Accessories

This chapter covers some of the additional equipment available for your video setup. You can shoot good, pleasing videos without these accessories, but having them can help ensure your results and increase your enjoyment of the finished product. We'll look at various types of filters, the lens hood, lens extenders, camera supports, specialized microphones, and supplementary lighting.

FILTERS

A *filter* reduces the amount of light reaching the lens. If the light source is too bright for the scene you're shooting, the solution is to cut down the light by placing a darker piece of glass over the lens. That's really the essence of what you have to know about filters for your outdoor videos.

There are many special-effects filters. You've probably seen what they can do as part of those high-budget commercials on television. They're used to alter the reality of a scene substantially and to get your attention—fast. There are starburst filters, multifaceted filters to produce kaleidoscopic effects, and filters to split images, to produce streaks or cross-hatch marks, to soften images to an ethereal state, and to affect color for a dreamlike vision. These filters are so specialized and so rarely used outside the commercial studio, though, that we don't need to detail them here. Besides, they're often used so badly they become distractions and clichés in video moviemaking.

The most useful filters for the vast majority of situations you'll encounter when shooting outdoor videos are the skylight filter, the neutral-density filter, the polarizing filter, and the amber and blue filters.

The Skylight Filter

The *skylight filter*, sometimes called a neutral-density 1-A (or 1-B) filter, should be the first accessory you buy for your video camera. This inexpensive filter, made of specially treated glass, effectively cuts down on excessive ultraviolet radiation from the sun to reduce glare and enrich the colors of the scene you shoot. It also protects the expensive lens of your camera from getting scratched; if the filter gets scratched, you can replace it easily. Once you get a skylight filter, screw it on the universal threads found on virtually every lens rim and forget it—it can stay there forever.

Neutral-Density Filters

Deeper-tinted *neutral-density filters* (sometimes called ND filters) are next on the list of accessories. At times, the bright sun can be so intense it overpowers the sensitivities of the video camera circuitry. This is when you reach for a neutral-density filter. Like good sunglasses, the neutral-density filters appear gray, but they don't affect the natural colors of the scenes you shoot. These filters are usually numbered #2, #4, and #8, but it's not necessary to stock up on all of them. In most instances, a #2 or #4 filter will block out sufficient light to do the job. A #2 reduces the light by 50 percent; a #4 reduces it by half again. A #8 filter is quite dark and will rarely be needed.

The Polarizing Filter

One more filter to consider is the *polarizing filter*. This is truly a spectacular filter to use when strong sun glare is a factor. Imagine a tranquil beach scene in the tropics with the brilliant sun angling across azure waters. The scene burns out, though, because of the brightness of the sun and the reflective glare off the water. A polarizing filter cuts through that glare and reflection to produce smooth, even-colored waters through which you might even see the sandy bottom. This filter also reduces glare overhead, darkening the blue of the sky and heightening the whiteness of the puffy clouds. The rest of the colors in your scene remain natural, just a little more vivid and intense. All in all, it's a grand effect.

Although polarizing filters tend to be more expensive than skylight filters and the neutral-density filters, they're well worth the money. The only drawback to using a polarizing filter is that the result is so interesting and pleasing, you might want to use it all the time. It can be habit-forming. With the exception of the skylight filter, which should remain on your lens, use filters sparingly—only when you have to and only when you want to create a certain effect. The rest of the time, allow nature to reveal her own special effects.

Amber and Blue Filters

Amber and blue filters are specialized filters that have some useful applications for outdoor videography. Both come in a variety of densities from a light tint to a deep hue.

Amber filters can warm a subject that is shaded by trees or that is reflecting cool blue or green light from another source. You can also use a very light amber filter when overcast skies give an unwanted feeling of coldness to a scene.

The *blue filter* is particularly handy when videotaping something indoors using incandescent lighting, such as regular table or floor lamps. The scene the camera sees without the filter will be quite warm, with an obvious yellow or even reddish light. The pale blue filter blocks the yellow and red light, rendering the scene more natural-looking to the eye. Outdoors, a darker blue filter can turn day to night, casting a bluish tint to your video scenes. The effect has been compared to moonlight.

These two filters are a little tricky to use properly, and it takes practice to achieve good results. Remember to remove the filter when the scene that required it changes and a new scene with different lighting characteristics is next on the shooting schedule.

LENS HOODS

An additional accessory to the camera lens is a *lens hood*, or what is sometimes called a lens shade. This is usually a built-in feature of the lens structure; if it's not, plan to buy one when you get the skylight filter. For outdoor videos, a lens hood is important because it shields the lens from extraneous glare and harsh side reflections. When you shoot in the direction of the sun, a lens hood enables you to shoot much closer to the position of the sun without getting zapped by direct rays. It also helps protect the lens from accidental bumps.

The lens hood is usually made of rubber or plastic and has a threaded base. On most cameras, it can stay on the lens, just over the protective skylight filter. Additional filters can be attached with the screw threads, and an external white-balance shield will sometimes fit right over the hood itself. This handy arrangement enables you to keep your important lens attachments on the lens, where they belong.

LENS EXTENDERS

Supplementary optics, called *lens extenders*, are important accessories to your video package. These extra lenses are generally available in sets of two: one for extra wide-angle shots, and the other for added telephoto effects. They're manufactured by several different companies, but most have universal threads so that they screw onto the rim of the camera lens. Before modern zoom lens construction was available for still photography, telephoto extenders and supplementary wide-angle lenses were common additions to film cameras. There's nothing new about these tools; they're just being adapted to video.

The average telephoto lens extender can boost the magnification power of your regular lens at least two to four times. At the other end of the scale, the wide-angle extenders can open up the scene you're videotaping to equal the peripheral range of your own eyes. One drawback to these accessories is that adding an extra lens to the existing lens lowers the optical quality somewhat. In some cases, with very good extenders, the degradation will be slight, perhaps unnoticeable to the average eye. With cheaper optics, you can readily see the difference in the viewfinder as you shoot. Before buying any extender, ask to try it out first.

Ideally, lens extenders should zoom along with the standard zoom lens on your camera. Some do, but some don't. Most telephoto extenders operate only at the high end of the zoom magnification scale, but new extenders are now being produced that offer full zoom capability.

Some of the leading manufacturers are releasing interchangeable lenses for their video cameras. The new lenses come right from the technology of 35mm film photography, and offer exciting prospects to the wildlife videographer who needs extra magnification and clarity to get videos of animals and shy birds in the wild. The Canon Company is leading this movement toward interchangeable lenses, but the lenses promise to be expensive and, for the immediate future, beyond the range of the beginning videographer. Sony appears to be sticking to fixed lenses and supplementary extenders.

A final caveat is in order. When using a telephoto extender, any camera movement will be transmitted to the video picture. The result might well be a shaky scene that is unusable. You can't hold a video camera with a long telephoto lens by hand and expect a clear set of images. This is where a tripod becomes a necessity.

CAMERA SUPPORTS

One of the major flaws in many home videos is the jiggly, jumpy image produced by camera movement. The problem is so easily corrected, it's surprising how common it is and how many people balk at dealing with it. The solution, of course, is to hold the camera steady, and the best way to do this is with a *tripod*.

Tripods have been a mainstay film camera accessory since the dawn of photography. Every photographer in the old days used a tripod or some other camera support because the old film and lens shutters were just not fast enough to allow for hand-held operation. We got out of the habit of using tripods when faster films were developed for the new compact cameras. When home-movie film cameras died out, most camera buffs buried their tripods alongside, never to be resurrected. Or so they thought. But along came video and even with good, modern equipment, most people once again started producing jiggly home movies.

The problem can't be traced to slow film speed—there's no film in video, just magnetic tape responding to electrical impulses, and the speed of videotape can't be measured the way the speed of film can. The problem comes from the wonderful advances in technology that produced the telephoto and zoom lenses we find on all video cameras. These lenses are so sensitive, they pick up little details at great distances and, by doing so, exaggerate every motion detected by the camera's sensors. You simply can't use a zoom lens to swoop in and record close-up detail without magnifying all the extra movements you're making, including any slight shaking in your hand as your muscles contract with tension while shooting.

This is where a tripod or some other steady support comes in, and the more you use one, the better your videos will be. It's a good habit to develop, but I'll concede it's not always convenient or easy to do. Once a tripod is set up, however, the rest of your video shooting can flow as smoothly as the movements of the tripod's head.

A good tripod has a lock-on head to fasten securely to the video camera body. The head itself should provide fluid, multidirectional action to allow for *tilt* (up-and-down movement), *panning* (side-to-side swing) and *cant* (pitch to one side or the other). A nice feature on many tripods is a quick-release camera base that can be threaded onto the video camera and left there. The camera and base can then be quickly clipped to, and unclipped from, the tripod itself. The ease of this attachment increases the chances the tripod will be used.

Other possibilities in camera supports include a small pocket-size tripod, which gives some additional stability for the camera when you're outside. You might use something like this when shooting from a dock or pier, or perhaps from the stands of an outdoor stadium. This tripod will find a score of uses if you give it a chance.

A *unipod* (also called a monopod) has been used successfully by many photographers and videographers. I find that it complicates my efforts in keeping the camera level and steady, but others swear by the design and praise its compact size and portability. I guess the choice is one of personal experience and taste. The bottom line on supports is to find one that works for you and then use it as much as possible.

The design of full-size video cameras virtually forces you to operate them as you would portable rocket launchers. They rest comfortably, more or less, on one shoulder and most of the important controls are within reach of the fingers of one hand—usually the one on the arm supporting the camera. Supplementary supports are now available for the camera that are form-fitted to your shoulder; they make holding a full-size video camera much more comfortable, improving camera stability at the same time. These shoulder mounts are designed along the lines of a rifle stock, or they might be a more simple inverted U-shaped piece that clamps to the camera. With either design, the objective is the same—to blend camera and body into one form, making you the vital support for the camera (see photo on page 6).

SPECIALIZED MICROPHONES

The built-in microphone on your video camera is a general-purpose, workhorse piece of equipment that solves your basic needs in recording the nearby sounds of the scenes you shoot. Whether mono or stereo, the most common microphone attached to the camera is the unidirectional *cardioid mike*. It's called a cardioid because the sound pattern it picks up is shaped like a heart. The sensitivity pattern bulges at the sides to flow outward to a central point. The cardioid mike concentrates its sound pickup from one general location. It's most sensitive straight ahead, with the sensitivity decreasing quickly at the sides. There's little, if any, sensitivity at the rear of the microphone. It's a good, basic microphone.

The mike is mounted on the camera because this makes a convenient, tidy package, though it's hardly the optimum position from which to record the sounds of any scene you shoot. To improve your sound recording, and to get more pertinent sound from your scenes, you must have a remote microphone pickup situated at the point of action. This means your camera should have an input jack to accommodate an extra mike. Many cameras now offer this option.

The remote mike usually feeds its signal to the camera via cable, which means that mike placement is limited by the length of the cable. An alternative, though not necessarily an improvement, is a wireless mike package, which includes a small VHF radio transmitter on the mike and a small receiver mounted on the camera and cabled to it through the external microphone jack. The distance of separation is still limited to 50 to 100 feet or so; beyond that, the audio signal begins to fade and break up. A better option for serious videographers might be a remote audio recording, which could be mixed with the video signal during editing (see Chapter 5).

There are three basic types of microphones: the unidirectional cardioid mike (described above), the multidirectional mike, and the shotgun mike.

The *multidirectional mike* has sound sensitivity all the way around in a circle; it picks up sound from any direction. At first this might appear to be a good feature, but the nonselectivity of this microphone limits its use to situations in which broad general sounds are desired. Plant this microphone in the middle of a circle of people or in a forest where sounds can come from any direction.

The *shotgun mike* has an extremely selective pattern of sound pickup. This mike is not like a shotgun at all, but more like a rifle pinpointing a specific and small target. The long length of a shotgun mike helps to pick up sound coming from one source only. It's useful when specific sounds must be isolated and amplified. For outdoor work, the shotgun mike has great possibilities for nature videos. Another

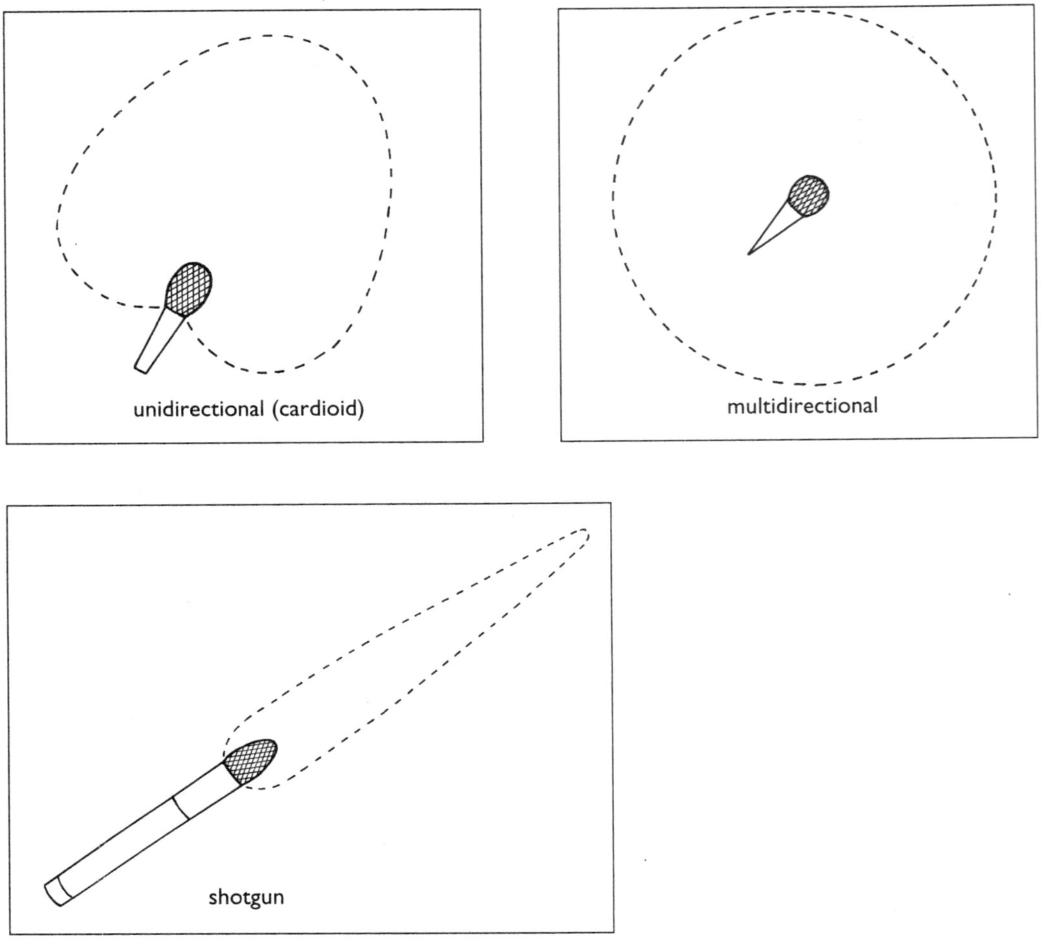

Specialized microphones with varying sound patterns include unidirectional or cardioid mikes, multidirectional mikes, and shotgun mikes.

good use for a shotgun mike is at sporting events, such as a football game when you want to isolate the quarterback calling out his signals at the snap of the ball. You see big-time versions of the shotgun mike when you watch football on TV. The sound technicians roam the sidelines with huge, long microphones that look like slender rifles inside metal beach umbrellas. These are highly sensitive, highly directional shotgun mikes. Without these microphones, the tremendous roar of the crowd would drown out all other sounds.

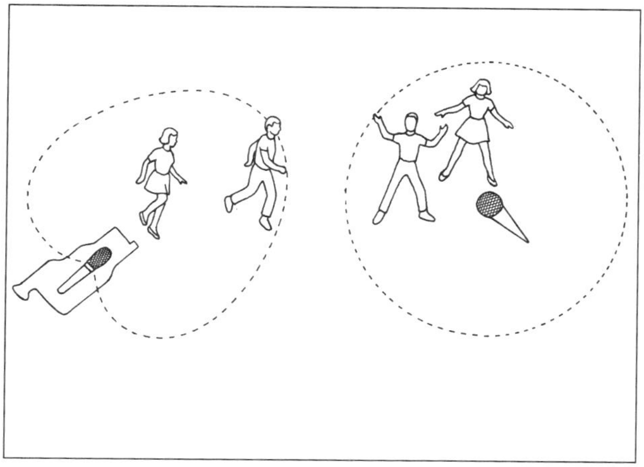

To pick up additional sound, you might combine a camera-mounted unidirectional mike with an external multidirectional mike.

SUPPLEMENTARY LIGHTING

In a book about outdoor videos, you would be correct in assuming that the emphasis would be on sunlight as the source of primary illumination, and it's true that the best light to shoot under is natural sunlight. But you should also give some thought to supplementary artificial lighting when the sun goes down, when it's obscured by heavy cloud cover, or when it's behind the subject you want to video.

The subject of artificial lighting is complex, because in order for the light to appear natural it must, in fact, be unnatural, even exaggerated. This is akin to the actor on stage having to speak louder, slower, and more dramatically so as to project a personality that is perceived by the audience as natural. Good artificial lighting technique can be considered an art. It must be practiced and perfected, because good results rarely come by accident.

With that in mind, let's look briefly at just one more accessory to the video camera: the external camera-mounted video light, which is secured to the camera with a clip (called a shoe). In my opinion, this is the worst light for videos, yet it's the first accessory recommended by most sales clerks and illustrated in the brochures.

Like the built-in microphone, the camera-mounted light is the wrong piece of equipment in exactly the wrong spot. The beam of light it casts is somewhat narrowly directed, and the light itself is harsh and flat. It's good only for a relatively short distance, so it intensely lights up the subject in the immediate foreground, leaving strong shadows and the rest of the background in darkness. In many ways, it works like a spotlight focused on a star performer on a theater stage. Unlike the spotlight, however, the little camera-mounted light can't be moved independently; it goes where you point the camera. Videos shot with this light often look as though they have been illuminated by an automobile headlight.

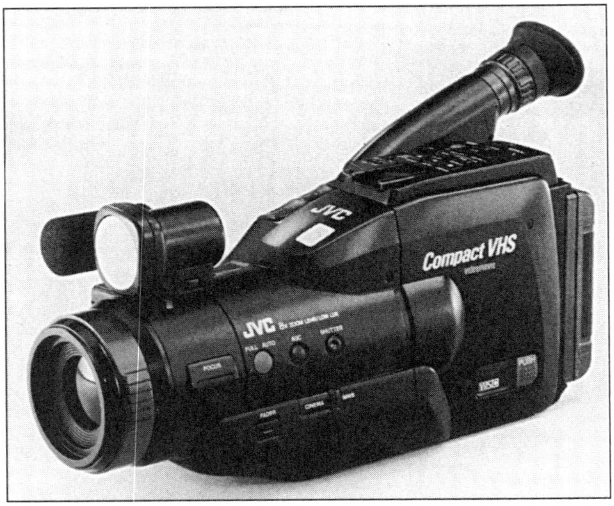

The advantages of a camera-mounted video light can outweigh the drawbacks if you have no other source of supplemental lighting. (Courtesy JVC)

On the other hand, any supplementary lighting is better than no light at all. A camera-mounted light designed for your particular camera is always better than something you make up yourself and then have to hold up with one hand while trying to balance the camera and shoot with the other. And it can be useful as a fill-in light to illuminate the subject when the sun is behind your subject or is otherwise obscured.

If nothing else, artificial lighting solves one problem inherent with natural light: control. With artificial lighting, such as floodlights and even the little camera-mounted light, you can pretty much control the light as you choose. Natural light can't be controlled; it must be dealt with. You must learn to adjust your shooting to accommodate that light. That requires some understanding of light itself—what it is and what it can do. And that's what we're going to look at next.

CHAPTER THREE

Technique and Composition

So far, we've looked at the standard and optional equipment available to the new videographer. Now we can move on to the real nitty-gritty: understanding the properties of light and color, planning an interesting video, using basic techniques to create exciting and lively shots, and applying the principles of good composition that will make your productions pleasing to look at and seamless.

UNDERSTANDING LIGHT AND COLOR

Light makes vision possible. In physics, light is defined as electromagnetic radiation occurring in different wave lengths. You don't have to understand the physics of light to shoot good videos, but you do need to know that light makes it possible to record images on electromagnetic videotape. The light source can be natural (from the sun) or artificial (light intentionally placed by the camera operator or stadium floodlights at sporting events).

There are several kinds of artificial light. Two very familiar sources of artificial light found in the home are incandescent and fluorescent bulbs. For video, television, movies, and photography, there are also special studio lights made of a variety of materials, including tungsten, that cast all kinds of hues and render different results.

The Color of Light

We generally think of light as colorless or, at best, white. It's something neutral that shines down on objects to reveal their individual colors. Light, we imagine, illuminates the green grass, the red flower, or the blue sky. Well, it doesn't work that way.

Light is actually made up of many colors, some of which are absorbed by objects, others of which are reflected. The color we see is actually the light reflecting off an object and bouncing back to us. Green leaves, for example, reflect the color green in the rays of light shining on them; the leaves absorb most of the other colors, so all we see is green.

Think of the spectrum of color you see when a band of light is bent, or *refracted*, through a prism. A rainbow is a natural spectrum occurring when a beam of sunlight is refracted through atmospheric moisture. With a bit of luck we can see the full spectrum: broad bands of red, orange, yellow, green, blue, and violet.

What we consider natural or colorless light is the blending together of all these separate colors. Thus, light is not color*less* but actually color-*full*. Dawn's pale early light is different from the hot tones of a tropical sunset. The light filtering through a leafy tree at midsummer is cool and green, quite in contrast with the cold blue light reflecting off a new snowfall in winter, or the warm yellow light radiating from a sandy beach under the spell of the summer sun. Indoors, fluorescent lights generally give off a cool, bluish light, while regular incandescent bulbs glow warmer with a distinctly yellowish light.

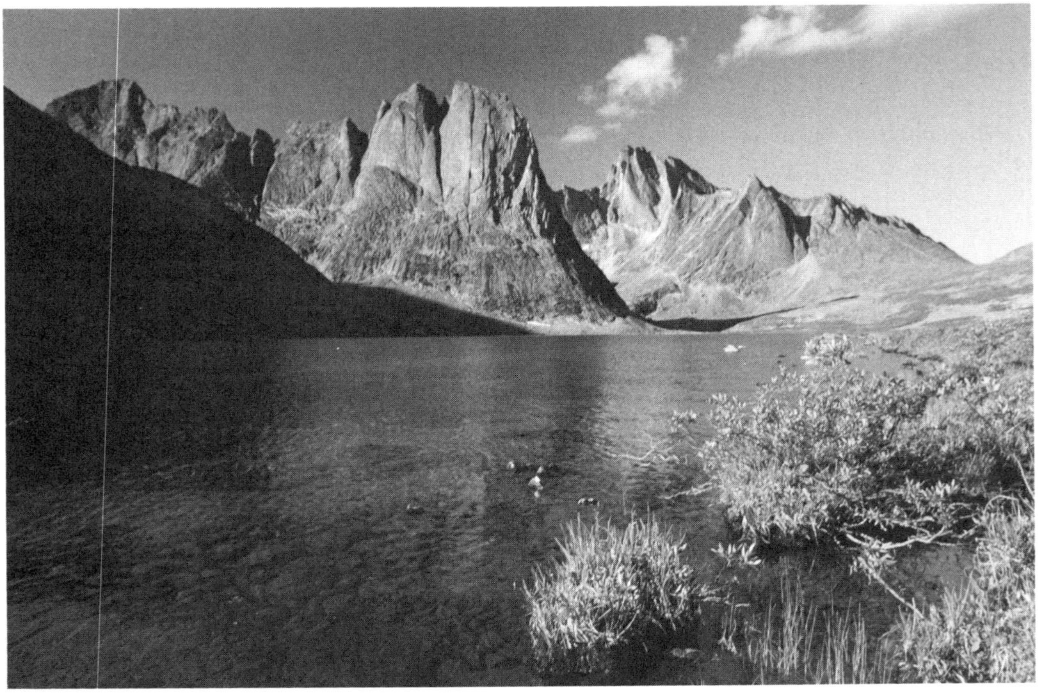

Though it would make a nice cutting shot, a static scene like this always looks better in person than it does on the screen.

So, visible light actually comes in a variety of colors depending not only on its source, but also on how it is reflected. Our eyes and brain compensate for slight differences in the colors of light to give us the impression of neutral or, in video terms, *white* light.

Unlike our eyes, the electronic sensors in the video camera can't always discern these differences and then compensate quickly enough to emulate neutral white light. It becomes necessary, therefore, to make this adjustment for the camera. This compensation is known as correcting the white balance.

In Chapter 1, I mentioned that your video camera automatically corrects for different light conditions, but that you should also have some way to make this correction manually. It's worth repeating because this is probably the most important camera control you'll use when making your videos; in effect, it directs the camera to see the light as you see it. Use it often, even if you have automatic settings.

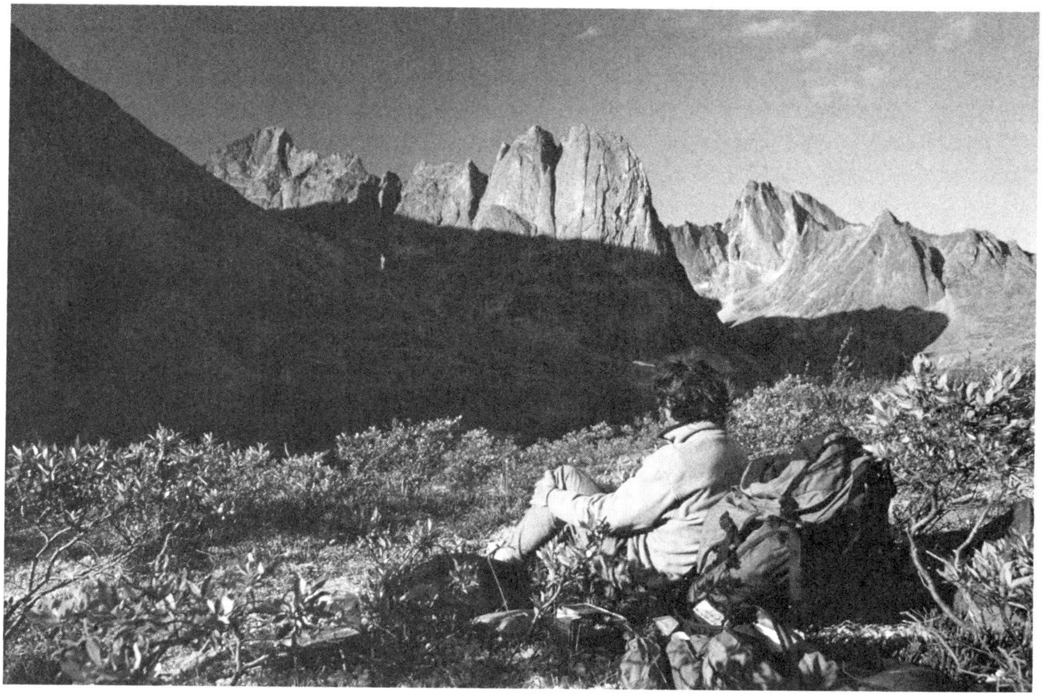

Here the hiker gives purpose to the scene and provides a better sense of the size and scope of the mountains. Unfortunately, the camera's light sensors were fooled by the brightness of the sun and sky. The deep shadows indicate that other parts of the picture are underexposed. It's a tough call: If you open the aperture to bring in more light, the hiker will be overexposed. The best compromise might be to wait until the sun is shining from the proper angle, illuminating the mountains.

Make it a habit to correct the white balance before each scene you shoot and immediately after shooting toward any strong light source—especially the sun or the glare off sand or snow. Most color problems and color flare-ups you see in amateur videos are the result of not making this simple correction whenever light conditions change.

The Best Time to Shoot

I noted earlier that sunlight is the best illumination for most outdoor videography. You'll get the best and most natural colors outdoors if you shoot during daylight hours, approximately two hours after sunrise until about two hours before sunset. This doesn't mean that sunrise or sunset pictures won't have their own special impact; they will. Good scenes shot at these times can be spectacular, but videos shot when the sun is too close to the horizon often carry a reddish tint. If the scene is too dark and the sun is below the horizon, your videos might have an excessively bluish cast. It's much better to shoot your videos later in the morning when the light is soft and gentle, or in the afternoon when shadows are lengthening and the light is somewhat warmer. Your videos will be richer in color and detail. Avoid shooting videos at high noon, however, when the sun is directly overhead. The noonday sun casts deep shadows that fall like a dark mantle over people and things, projecting a harsh, flat light that is unflattering to almost every subject.

Never shoot right into the sun, and never look straight at it either. The direct rays of the sun can easily burn your eyes and damage the electromagnetic sensors inside the camera. You can still get those memorable sunsets and other sun scenes by shifting the camera's center of focus slightly to one side of the sun. The beauty of the setting sun is in the clouds and sky, not in the flaming disk itself.

Videotape is generally more forgiving than photographic film, and it can be used in a wider range of existing light conditions. Just keep in mind that there is a limited amount of time available to shoot after the sun sinks below the horizon. Not even modern videotape and electronic sensors can record images in total darkness.

During daylight hours, the most difficult conditions to shoot under are broken patches of bright sun and deep shadows. Most of the time, the electronic sensors inside the camera make the necessary adjustments, but occasionally the light changes so fast the camera can't adjust quickly enough. The result is flare or sudden bursts of darkness on the screen. You can see for yourself how this broken daylight affects sports coverage on TV when late-afternoon shadows obscure portions of the sun-filled playing fields.

One key to resolving the dilemma of drastically changing light conditions is to anticipate them. As the videographer and director of your own movie, you have the opportunity as well as the responsibility to anticipate what your next scene might include. Look around to see if any deep shadows will obscure your shooting, or if a bright burst of sunlight cuts into the deep shade where you plan to shoot next. Try to avoid areas of strongly contrasting light values so that your videos are more evenly lighted. Also, when shooting in areas where the light changes abruptly, anticipate the change by manually adjusting the aperture—opening it as you go from light to dark, and closing it as you go from dark to light.

Perhaps the best conditions for outdoor videos come when shooting under open shade—any situation in which a large shadow covers the entire subject. The shadow of a building, for example, casts an even, soft, flattering light. Similar conditions exist when the sun doesn't fully cooperate and you're faced with an overcast day or even the threat of rain. This is not the time to put away your video camera in disappointment. A bright, overcast day often produces just the right conditions for memorable videos. You've probably already seen this phenomenon and not even been aware of it. In autumn, for example, when the northern hardwood forests are ablaze with crimson and golden leaves—or as we now know, when those leaves are reflecting shades of red and yellow light—we see the most vivid colors under the subdued lighting of overcast skies. There's no harsh competition from the intense light of the sun. We see the light properly reflected, without glare or shadow. So keep your video camera handy for some memorable scenes on otherwise dull days.

PLANNING MAKES PERFECT

"Film is cheap, but good pictures are priceless," a successful commercial photographer once told me. "Shoot as much as you can. The editing will sort it all out."

Those are good words for any photographer or videographer to remember, but the trained eye of the professional is different from the hopeful eye of the beginner. Unless you plan before you shoot, use discipline while you shoot, and edit carefully after you shoot, your videos will be endless yards of inaction without a meaningful story to be told. You must always be thinking of ways to shorten your story, to tighten it up and make it lively.

Many years back, when I was a beginning photojournalist for a local TV news show, I was given a 16mm motion-picture film camera, two 100-foot rolls of film, and instructions to go out and cover my news assignment and anything else that developed. When I returned to the station at the end of the day to write up my story, I turned over the exposed film to a darkroom technician for processing. It was my job to do the final film editing later for the broadcast.

I was actually allowed as much film as I needed, but the station owner was particularly strict about waste. He hated it. If any of us reporters came in with an excessive amount of exposed film, we usually heard from the boss. We were instructed to keep the ratio of film shot to film used to approximately 2-to-1 (2 feet of film exposed to 1 foot edited for use on the air). It was a hard rule to follow, and it was a bit overzealous.

The harshness of that rule was underscored for me during one assignment when I ran into a film crew from the British Broadcasting Company. I was a one-man band; they numbered eight. The leader of the BBC crew remarked to me that they were on a severe budget cut that permitted them only a 50-to-1 shooting ratio (50 feet shot, 1 foot used). Some months earlier, they had been shooting a documentary film in Australia. The budget had been much more realistic then, he said: 200-to-1!

I never made it to the BBC level, but my own shooting improved greatly as a result of the strict limit placed on us for film. We all shot good news footage, planned ahead as much as possible, figured out what we needed to tell the story, and edited "in the camera" as much as possible. We did this not only to save film, but also to save time at the editing table when we were faced with nightly broadcast deadlines.

Three key lessons remain in my mind today when I shoot videotape: plan what you want to shoot, shoot selectively, and then edit effectively. I'll cover the first two lessons in this chapter; editing, I'll save for Chapter 5.

Start with a Plan

I recall a stage play that starred Alec Guinness as a blind, somewhat tyrannical father. Each time his son came home, the father would want to know what he had been up to. He was not content with his son's simple explanations or his statement, "I wasn't doing anything special." Everything the boy did was special to his sightless father, who would lean back in his chair and say, "Paint me a picture." In making a video movie, it's your job to paint a picture of the event, to bring it across in a lively fashion to those who were not there.

Let's take a situation and see how we can plan a video movie. Your son or daughter is playing in a league soccer match this Saturday and you want to videotape the game. The weather forecast is favorable, your star player is in good spirits, and you and your friends are enthusiastically anticipating an exciting afternoon at the game. That's a simple scenario, but it's not so simple that you can allow the game itself to dictate your shooting. Don't just pick up your video camera as you walk out the door and think, "I'll shoot the game." This is the time for planning—what we call developing a story line—and you begin by outlining your video objectives.

In this example, unless you're making a training video to improve your child's performance, your objective should be to tell the story of the soccer game. This might include the family getting ready to leave for the game, the pageantry and excitement of events at the site, the companionship of your friends and other spectators, and the closeness of your child's teammates. These are your objectives. The next step is to think about what visual images you need to demonstrate each idea:

Preparation: Your child in the team uniform; family members piling into the car; the car pulling out of the driveway.

Pageantry: The stands filling with spectators; the players walking onto the field in clean uniforms; everyone singing the national anthem; the referee tossing the coin.

People: Friends arriving at the game; the fans cheering; the players' reactions after an exciting play; hugs of victory or of defeat.

Game: The first play; the officials controlling the game; the action of the game itself (keep your eyes open for an offbeat shot, perhaps of the goalie when his or her goal is not threatened).

Now within this broad outline, consider secondary images that might be useful to fill in the story line. These secondary images, called *cutting shots* (or cutaway shots), are short scenes you can use later when editing to bridge the longer sequences. (I'll talk about cutting shots in more detail later in this chapter.) Shots of the scoreboard at the beginning of the game, at the end of each quarter, as goals are scored, and at the end of the game reflect the game's progress. Close-ups of players and spectators reveal reactions to big plays. Have you thought to include the cheerleaders? Is there a team mascot? Shoot the crowd reaction for your team both when they're happy and when they're worried. Think of what distinguishes this particular game from others you've seen. Is it the team uniforms? Is it the size of the opposing players? Is it the field of play? Capture it visually. Move around the field. Forget the game for a while and think about individual pictures, images, impressions. Get a good variety of these cutting shots to lend impact to your finished video.

So now you have a good idea of the many visual images that would be exciting to see in your video. But they're all in a jumble. Plan just a little more, and you can record these images with as little postproduction editing as possible. How? Create a story board.

Create a Story Board

A *story board* is nothing more than a written plan of your story line. It doesn't have to be a complicated document. Just sketch out your plan in whatever manner appeals to you, maybe script form or standard outline form. I use 3 x 5 index cards. Use one for each image you plan to shoot. If you have artistic talent, you might even draw simple pictures on the cards to produce a visual story board. Or, you might want to jot down a few words of narration, or perhaps make note of some background music to add during editing. If you later shoot something not covered by a card, make up another card. When you finish the shooting, you might have a dozen or more cards, each with a little scene summary.

The cards help you in two ways: First, they provide a guide to what scenes to shoot; later, you can use the cards as an editing tool to help you sort and rearrange the various scenes for the most pleasing order in your finished production. The important thing is to think about your video in visual terms, to "see" your video before you shoot it. If you know what you want to record, the actual shooting will go much easier and the postproduction work of editing will be that much simpler.

Shoot Selectively

It's always tempting to pick up your video camera, aim it at your subject, and record every movement. It's particularly appealing when the subject happens to be a family member—a child performing well at sports or, even more compelling, the day you discover your baby can walk. Unless you want a lengthy video record of the event gathering dust in the family archives, resist the urge to shoot it all. Five or six baby steps edited into a broader family outing that includes others reacting to the event will be more appreciated over the years. No one ever willingly sat down to an entire evening devoted to the first two-and-a-half hours baby found his or her legs.

The same lesson applies to shooting outdoor sports. Take a baseball game: It's the bottom of the ninth inning, bases loaded, two outs, and the home team is behind by three runs. A double will likely tie the score, a home run will win the game and the championship. A power hitter is at the plate. You're in the stands, and the camera is ready. This is as dramatic and appealing a situation as ever confronted a home videographer. The first impulse is to press the record button and "let 'er rip." It's also probably the worst thing you can do.

Let's imagine the worst. For the next 10 minutes or so, the pitcher and the batter engage in a mind-numbing duel featuring a pitch, a foul ball hit out of play, another pitch, another foul. The pitcher pauses, the batter steps out of the box. The manager walks to the mound. The batter calls time out. This goes on and on while you dutifully record every blink and arm wave from a static position. Eventually, the big pitch comes and the batter swings for the fences. Your camera blinks a tiny warning light indicating the batteries have just expired or the videotape has run its length.

Never happen, you say? But it has, and it will, just when you don't want it to. So how do you avoid this catastrophe? The first and easiest way is to make doubly sure you have enough tape for the shoot and that your batteries are fully charged. That, at least, gives you the necessary tools for the job at hand. But that still doesn't give you a viewable video, one that not only captures all the action, but does it in a reasonable time span so you and others will want to see it again. Success depends on planning and anticipation.

Since the picture you really want is the batter winning the game, concentrate on getting that shot. Yes, you'll have to record all the pitches and all the foul balls, because any one of those pitches could be the one that gets hit out of the park to win the game. But the other parts of the game, which serve only to lessen the impact of the dramatic ending, can be eliminated through selective shooting. Stay alert when the manager confers with the pitcher or when the batter calls time out. Shoot perhaps a second or two of either incident, which might be useful in an editing session later. When another interruption occurs, use that time to record five seconds of crowd action, which you might also use.

After editing all the extraneous scenes, your video will be more like the highlights film presented each night on TV: a well-planned summary of the action adding to the drama of sport. Almost all your outdoor videos can benefit from this lesson in using anticipation, patience, and discipline to edit periods of inaction.

SHOOTING TECHNIQUES

Technique refers to the procedures and methods you use to shoot your videos: how to move the camera, how to vary your shots, and how to add sound and narration to your work.

Basic Camera Actions

Action is the key word for good videos, just as it is for good movies. Without it, all you have are static pictures that are better left for your still camera. Action can originate from several sources. People in motion produce the best action for videos, but there are a few camera-movement techniques that give the illusion of action and enhance your video production.

For most practical considerations, there are only four basic camera movements: zoom, pan, tilt, and shake. The first three are intentional and effective; the fourth, shake, is neither. So let's begin by looking at how shake can affect your videos.

Shake

Shake is defined as unwanted camera movement, a problem you create and something you must learn to avoid as much as possible. The first defense against shake is a tripod or other support (several were mentioned in Chapter 2). If you don't have a formal camera support, use what's available and learn to hold the camera as still as possible.

EDITING WITH THE CAMERA

Postproduction editing is the process of reassembling all the various pieces of audio and video information into a coherent story. But by being selective with what you shoot and when you shoot it, you can effectively edit with the camera while you record the scenes.

The first real editing decision you make is when to start recording. Every time you push the record button, you are selecting which scenes to shoot and what sequence they will follow. It might be terribly obvious, but the next important editing decision is when to stop recording. You can make these two basic in-camera editing choices confidently because you planned ahead and prepared a good story board on 3 x 5 index cards.

Now comes an in-camera editing technique that requires a bit more planning: recording cutting shots exactly where they will appear in the final version. A final in-camera editing technique comes with the use of *fade-in* or *fade-out* (also called a dissolve). This involves starting or stopping the recording action while gradually adjusting the aperture to control the amount of available light. You can do this manually by turning the aperture settings on the lens, or allow the camera to do it automatically when you press the fade-in or fade-out switch.

The fade-in and fade-out are big, dramatic effects usually reserved for opening and concluding scenes. If you use them, do so sparingly so as to preserve their impact. Also, don't use them on the spur of the moment, because the effect can't be removed.

Take a lesson from rifle target shooters, who must keep their weapons rock steady or miss the target. If you're hand-holding the camera, brace yourself with both feet wide apart. If a convenient post, the corner of a building, or a tree is nearby, lean against it. Keep both arms tucked in, elbows close to your body for added support. When you are ready to shoot, take a deep breath, let it all out, wait a second, and flip the switch. Now you're shooting smooth videos. The first few times you try this technique, you'll come up a little short of breath. Stick with it. Your ability to control your breath will improve with practice, and soon it will become almost second nature.

If your video plan calls for a low-level picture, get down where the action is. Don't simply aim your camera down—you won't be able to hold the camera steady, and you'll get an awkward view of your subject. Again, the old shooters' tricks for steadying the rifle come in handy. Try sitting down with your legs crossed or perhaps with your legs bent up and your elbows resting on your knees. Then, when you're steady, take a breath, let it out, wait a second, and shoot.

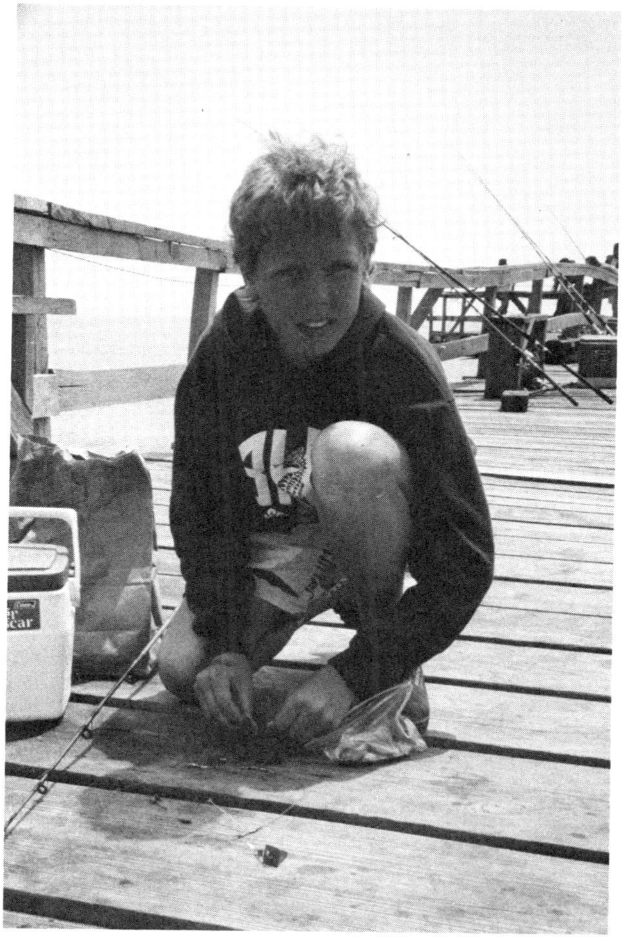

Children doing just about anything can be charming subjects for your home videos. For the best shots, get down at their level. You might even wind up shooting prone from ground level.

Zoom

Zoom, the first intentional camera movement we'll look at, refers both to the action and to the lens you use. Zooming is when you use the lens adjustment as you would a slide trombone to move your subject closer or farther away while everything remains in focus. Used judiciously, zooming is a dramatic technique that emphasizes the relative positions of your subjects. Because it's so exciting to use, though, zooming is usually overdone by the novice videographer. A video packed with zoom effects takes the audience on a dizzying roller coaster ride through the screen.

If you simply can't resist the magic of the zoom, try this technique to minimize the negative effects. Begin your scene with a close-up of your subject. Hold that shot

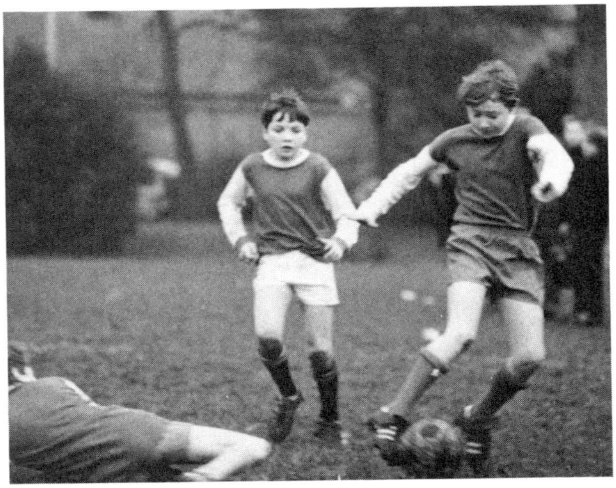

Imagine the effect of a reverse-zoom sequence at a soccer game. Begin with a close-up action shot of one player working the ball down the field, heading toward the camera. He avoids a tackle, outmaneuvers his opponents, and then kicks a powerful shot toward goal. Now, zoom out—either manually or by using the automatic switch—to reveal the flight of the ball toward the goal, the lunge of the goalie, and the other players' reactions. End the sequence with a pan of the crowd and a shot of the scoreboard.

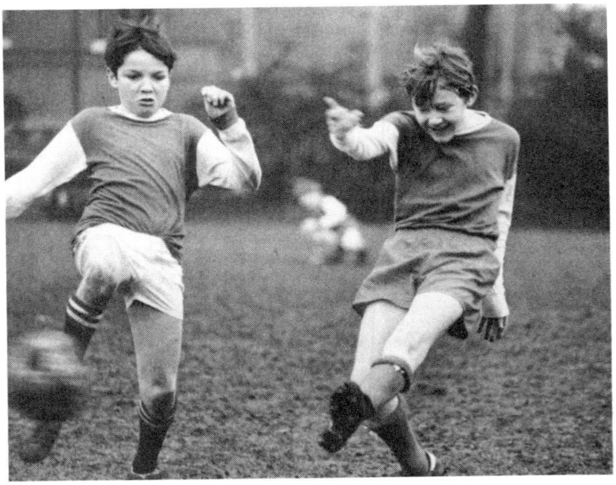

for three or four seconds to establish the scene. I call this my four-count rule. Then activate the automatic zoom or pull back the manual zoom to the desired wide-angle setting. Using this technique helps set the stage for unfolding events. You can demonstrate this yourself even without a camera. Cup one hand tightly and look through it as you would a telescope. Focus on something across the street from you, perhaps a building or a tree. Now slowly uncup your hand to reveal the expanding view. This is what the zoom does. Now go from the full wide-angle view (uncupped hand) to the close-up (cupped hand), and you'll see just how much more effective a *reverse* zoom sequence can be. It's also much easier to look at on the screen.

VARY THE ANGLE TO VARY THE SPEED

Want to make something appear to go faster than it's really going? Bring it close to the lens of the camera. Want to slow it down? Back away. Objects and people moving across the video screen appear to be going faster when they are close up, and slower when they are farther away.

Picture a speedboat racing across a lake. Up close, it whizzes by. But seeing it from a distance makes it appear slower because it takes much longer to move from one side of your field of vision to the other.

So, if you want to emphasize the speed of a runner in track-and-field events, shoot up close. To get a broader view of athletes in long-distance events, move back and let everyone get in the picture. That way you get a comparison of each runner's speed and more time to analyze the race.

Another interesting technique to use is angle shooting. Action shot obliquely appears slower than the same action viewed at right angles. Shoot an action scene moving away from the camera, and it will appear to be going at a slower speed than will the same action moving toward you.

Pan

Panning is when you move the camera from side to side in a sweeping motion to encompass a broad field of vision. Think of the word *pan* as short for *panorama* because it produces a panoramic view of the scene before you. Panning is a great way for the audience to follow the action as it takes place: a skier gliding down a mountain trail, or a race car speeding around the track.

Although almost everyone uses pan shots to establish the setting, they generally don't work well, especially long sweeping shots of the horizon. The camera simply can't edit visual material the way the human eye can. It can't discern and discriminate among the many images it picks up as you sweep across a landscape. The problem with pans comes from shooting too quickly and including too much material. Although the individual images might be clear, the result is a blur of video information.

Developing restraint with the pan is just about as difficult as holding back on zooms, but again, there's a simple trick to maximizing the good while minimizing the bad. Remember my four-count rule. Focus on something and hold your shot for about four seconds. Then slowly, very slowly, begin the sweep covering no more than 90 degrees (one-quarter of the way around a circle). Finish your shot by focusing again on something still. Hold that shot for another long four count. The silent four-count is very important. It should start and end all your shooting sequences. It forces you to concentrate on one scene at a time, and it helps greatly when editing because it gives you a cushion of tape in which to join scenes.

When shooting a pan, plant your feet first in the direction where the action is likely to end, and then pivot your body back to where the action will start. This way, both the action and the movement of the camera will match and be smooth. If you find yourself twisting and stretching your body back to where you want to start taping, you're probably trying to pan too wide an area. For best results, stay within the 90-degree range.

Tilt

A vertical pan—moving the camera up and down to emphasize height or depth—is called a *tilt*. Like the pan and the zoom, tilt is often overdone. It's also not a natural way of looking at things, so it's a technique best left for occasions when a particular effect is desired. If you decide to incorporate a tilt shot, remember the four-count rule to give your audience a frame of reference, and move the camera slowly so that the images don't blur together.

Getting Professional Results

Commercially made movies all contain sophisticated camera techniques and movements you just can't duplicate with limited home equipment. Still, there are some basic techniques you can adapt to improve the quality of your videos.

Learn to vary your shots. Mix wide-angle scenes with medium and short shots. Change positions to get better angles. If you're dealing with children at play, get down and shoot at their level. If you're shooting a football or soccer game, take your camera behind the goal line rather than remaining on the sidelines. Think about the amount of time you want to spend on each shot. Vary the time, but remember to allow a few extra seconds at the beginning and end of each sequence to allow for possible editing. Even if your scene doesn't need additional work, the extra time at each end is useful padding that will help your viewers identify the scene and become involved.

Above all, people make the difference. Shoot people in action and you'll be well on your way to a good video. Position your subjects where you want them, but don't pose them. Let people move freely and naturally. They're not trained actors, and chances are you haven't studied the ways directors get people to move in exactly the way they envision. So let your subjects find their own movements. With some luck, they'll soon forget the camera is trained on them. Even outdoors, with wonderful scenery in every direction, your videos will benefit from the human-interest factor.

Ken Burns, producer-director of the magnificent epic television series "The Civil War," noted that television, and therefore video, is inherently an intimate medium. The perfect number for the small screen is 2 people, not 20. So shoot small, shoot intimate, shoot detail, and shoot close-ups rather than wide-angle views.

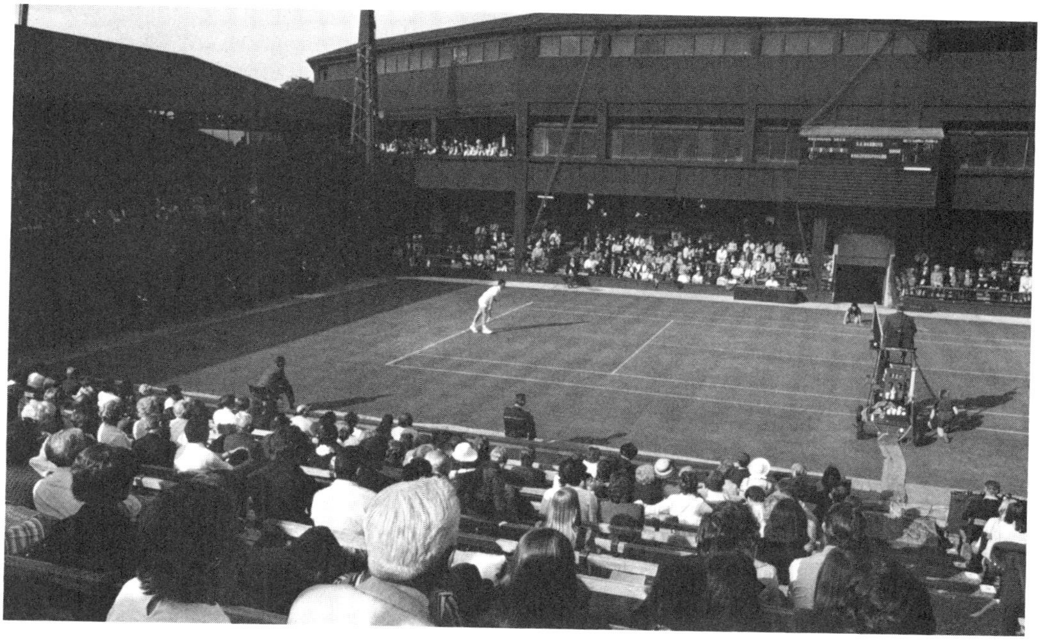

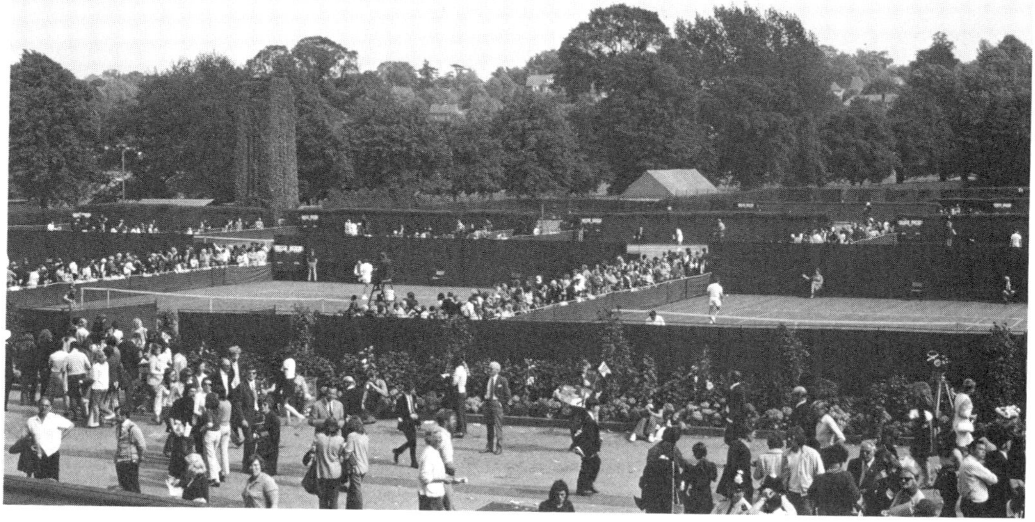

A good establishing shot for a tennis match can come from high up in the stands. Vary your angle and position as the match progresses.

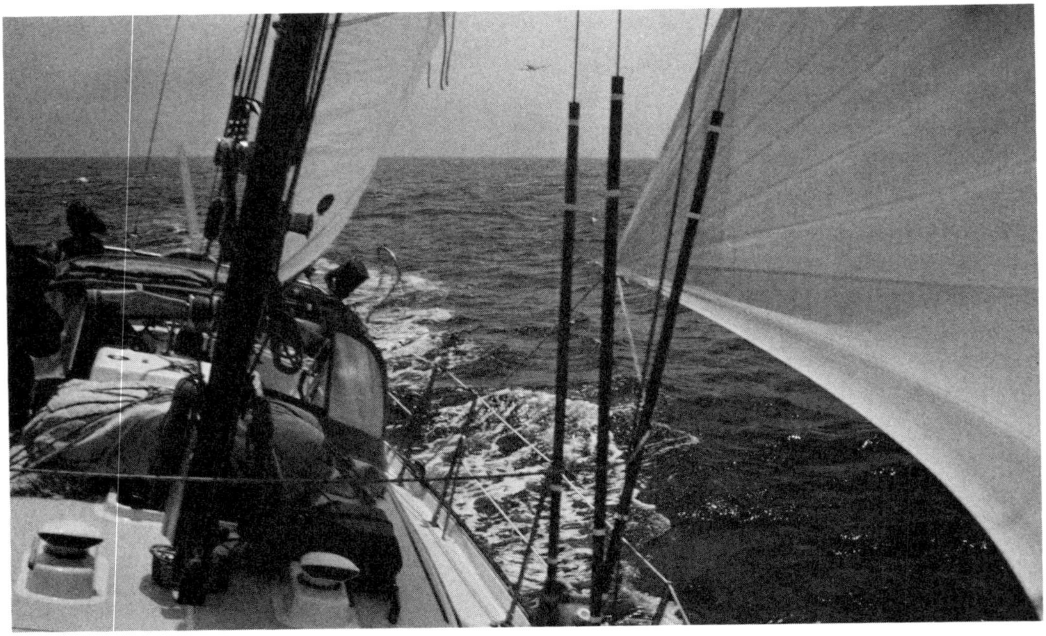

A common sailboat scene takes on new interest when shot from the bow.

The nice thing about video is that it's so forgiving. You can practice your shots over and over again with a variety of subjects under differing conditions. Since you can see the results in the viewfinder as you shoot, you can make adjustments as you go. You can even rewind the tape a bit to re-record a scene (whenever you record a scene over top of a previously recorded scene, the old scene is erased completely).

Keep notes on how you handled situations and refer to them often. What filter did you use to get that effect? How did you support the camera? What was the weather? Was there bright sun or clouds? What shots did you use? You'll soon become confident in your abilities so that when that next important scene comes along, you'll be ready.

SOUND AND NARRATION

The most underrated, widely misunderstood, and least appreciated component of any good movie is sound. Now that's a pretty strong statement, but think about it. When Al Jolson sang in "The Jazz Singer" to usher in the beginning of sound in motion pictures—the talkies—silent films were instantly relegated to second-rate status.

(text continued on page 53)

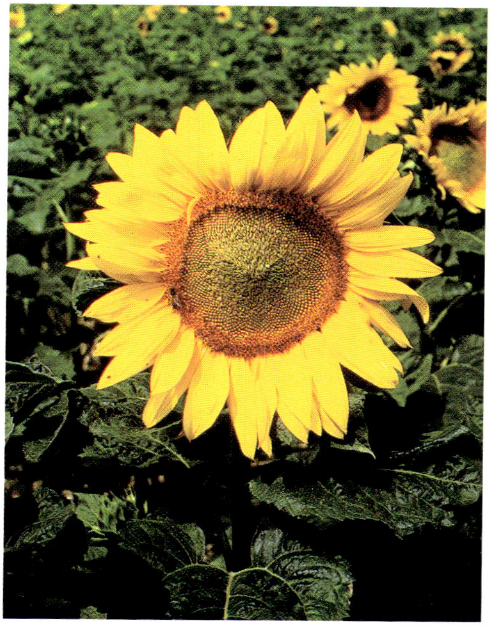

The macro setting is a wonderful feature found on many zoom lenses, allowing you to shoot close-ups of flowers and even tiny insects.

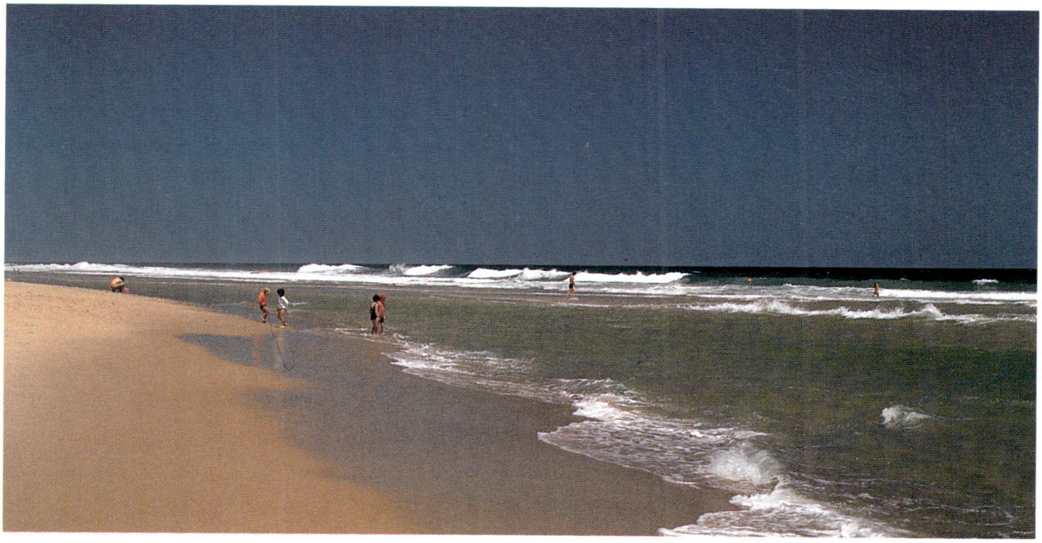

A polarizing filter substantially reduces the amount of light passing through the lens, so its value is realized most on bright, sunny days. In this shot, the filter virtually eliminates glare reflecting off the water and darkens the sand to a rich color of honey, while the sky becomes royal blue. White objects, in this case waves, are accentuated. Although the initial effect is pleasing, to be consistent you must retain the filter for all the scenes in a video sequence.

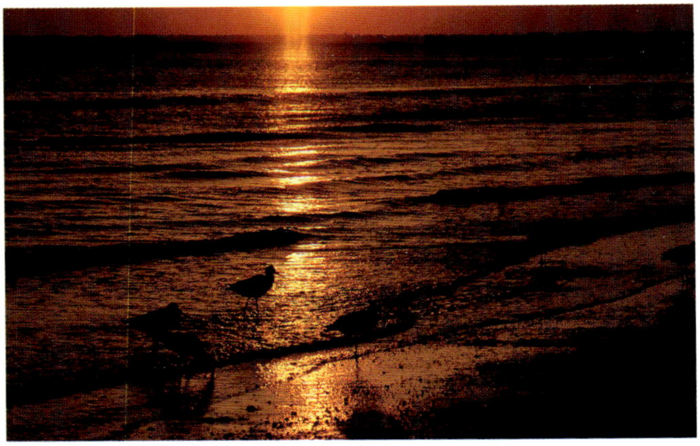

Sunsets are favored subjects of photographers, and videographers are equally enthralled. But watching a prolonged video of the setting sun can seem like an eternity to your audience; it's better to make sunset scenes brief. Shoot just as the sun is about to dip below the horizon, when the color is most vivid and while the glare and harmful rays are minimized. Whenever possible, get people into your videos. A couple walking along the beach as the sun goes down adds interest to the scene. The shore birds come back now, especially if the tide is low. Their calls will be picked up by the microphone and will add another dimension to your video. Does your camera have an audio and video fade feature? This makes a natural conclusion to your video. In motion-picture parlance, it's called "fading to black."

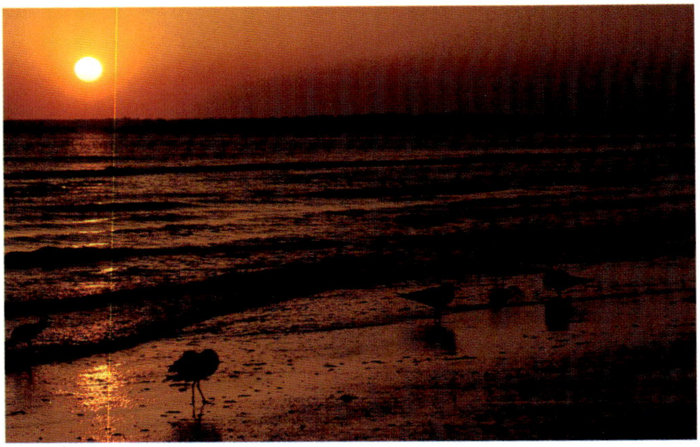

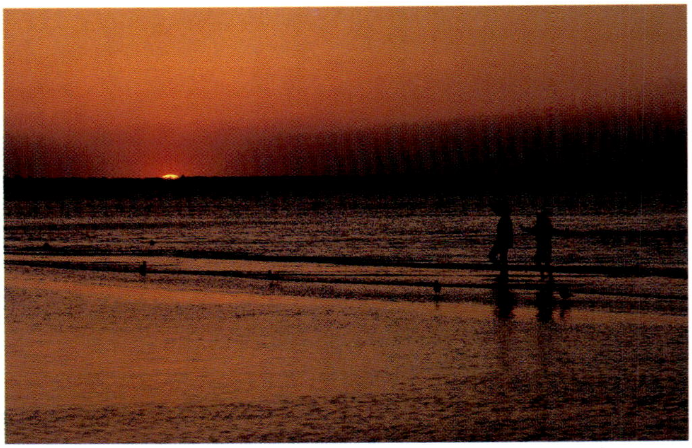

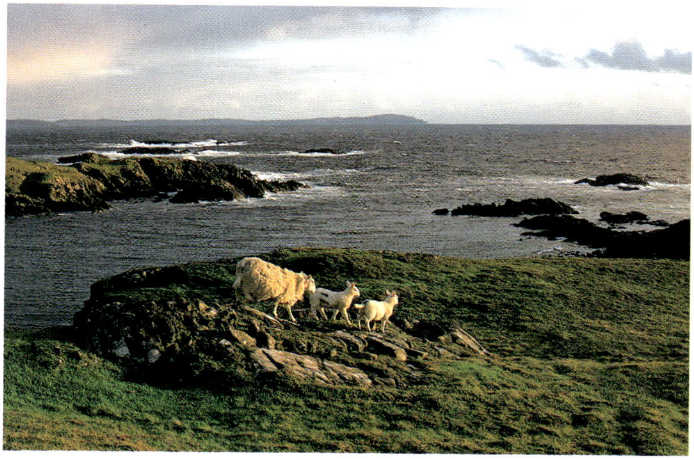

Can you see the rule of thirds applied here? Break this picture into thirds—vertically as well as horizontally. From bottom to top, the picture contains three elements: the ground, the sea, and the sky. Each occupies roughly the same amount of space. But what about thirds from side to side? This is more difficult to appreciate, but the rocky headlands at the left are counterbalanced by the sheep that are moving to the right and down the sloping meadow. Perhaps there's a crofter's cottage just out of the picture to the right. A slow, careful pan will show the cottage in the next scene and, at the same time, reveal a breathtaking vista of the Scottish coastline.

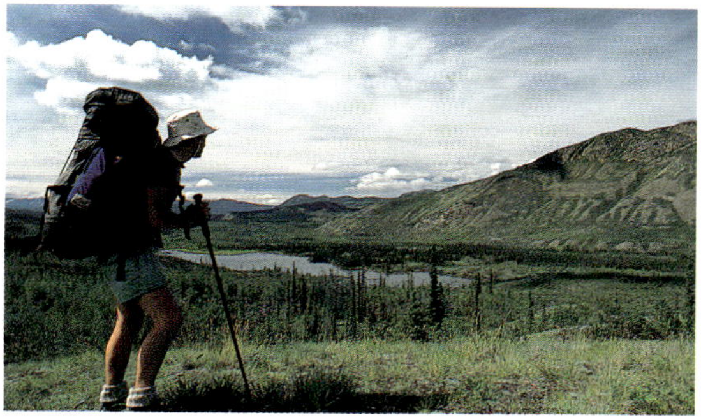

The sun, although relatively high in the sky, illuminates this scene nicely from the side. The hiker looks toward the mountains in the distance, and your eye is drawn to the far horizon. Now you can pan to the right to take in the full view. (Courtesy Chris Townsend)

Here's some unusual framing. A rooftop in Bermuda occupies a major portion of this scene. The light and color are interesting, and the slope of the roof leads your eye to the harbor below. This is a nice way to introduce waterfront activities, but it's too bad the sailboat is moving to the left. As it continues out of the picture, its motion will be at odds with the direction your eye is following along the roof line.

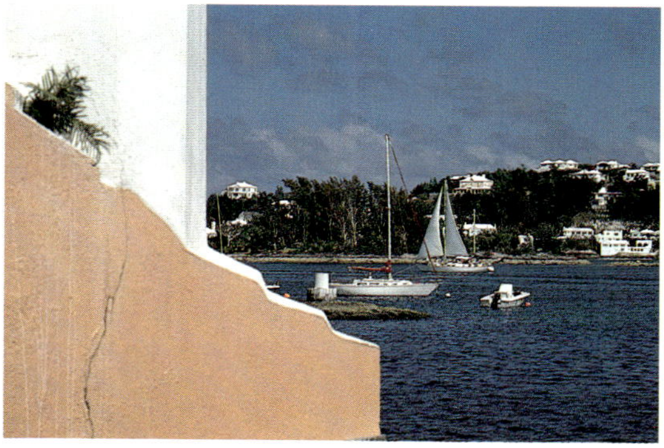

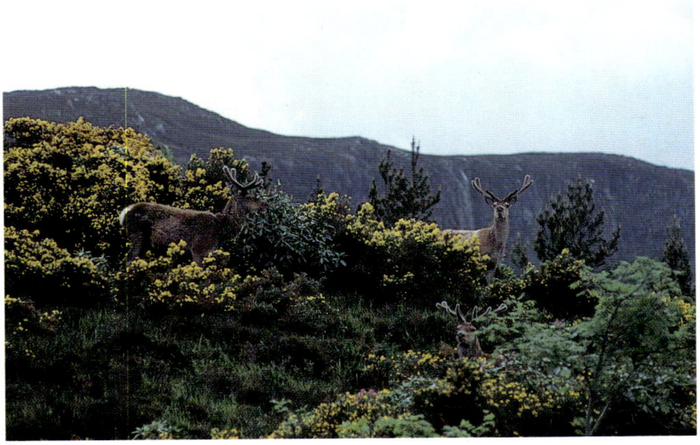

These Scottish Highland stags on a hillside of gorse (a Scottish prickly plant) blend into the background and keep a safe distance from human intruders. The standard zoom lens of your video camera can't reach far enough to capture these elusive animals, but a telephoto lens extender would double the effective range of your shots. On some select but high-priced video cameras, interchangeable lenses permit the use of extra-power telephoto lenses that previously were available only for still cameras.

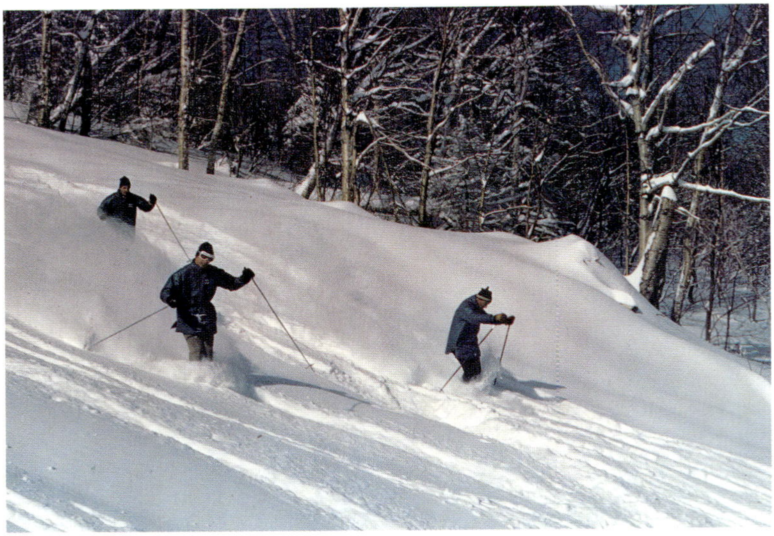

Capture all the excitement of a great day of skiing. The bright sun is well positioned about 45 degrees to the left of the camera. The shadows are strong, but not overpowering. The afternoon angle reduces glare, but the light illuminates the skiers' faces. The contrast between the blue sky and the white snow is echoed in their parkas. Their speed is shown by the flying plumes of snow. The apparent horizon is at a 45-degree angle, but the actual horizon is straight, as proved by the trees in the background. All in all, this is a pleasing shot with good composition and good action. Your decision as the videographer is whether to follow the skiers down the mountainside or let them ski out of the picture while the next skier approaches. If the former, remember the rules of panning: Plant your feet in the direction you'll be facing at the end of your shoot. As the skiers come down the trail, match your motions with their speed.

But even the old silent films had background sounds, usually a musical score played on a piano at the foot of the stage. The point is that movies and videos both benefit from the addition of related sound. Good sound, properly recorded and skillfully edited, can make a good movie great. But that's not easy to do with the standard sound equipment found on home video cameras.

Recording the Best Sound

Most cameras have a built-in microphone mounted right on the top. It looks nice, but it's probably the worst possible location. In that spot, most mikes are sensitive enough to pick up any sound the operator makes, as well as the sounds of the automatic zoom lens. The voice of the camera operator booms out, while the subject's voice, coming from as far as 15 to 20 feet away, varies in intensity as the microphone adjusts to pick up new sound. Turn the camera away to follow some new action, and you also turn the microphone away from the primary sound source.

Perhaps the biggest problem in recording sound for outdoor videos comes from wind noise. The built-in microphone is so far away from the subject that even a gentle breeze turns into a roar. *Wind socks* (little socks or booties of foam material that slip over the microphone) dampen the wind effect, but they also muffle other, more desirable sounds. A similar problem arises when you activate the microphone's sound-dampening switch (available on some models): both good and bad sounds are reduced. Technology is improving, though, and the negative effects are being countered. Some recently released models are capable of sensing wind noise and eliminating it.

There is another way around this problem, fortunately, and it requires no additional outlay of cash and no complicated adjustment of delicate equipment. The best way to avoid unwanted, disturbing sound is to disconnect the microphone. A contradiction, you say? First I say that sound is one of the most important facets of video, and then I say to disconnect the mike. Well, why not?

If the sound you're getting isn't any good for your finished video, why record it in the first place? Eliminate extraneous bad sound and either add new sound later or bring in narration over the silent tape to give it more impact. Certain videos, and especially certain scenes, benefit from being shot without sound.

Look and listen carefully to TV programs and movies to see if you can determine how the sound was recorded and how different sounds might have been added to produce the finished product. Shooting videos without sound is not widely used by the home moviemaker, but it's worth considering. Experiment.

Whenever you pick up your camera to record a scene, think of sound as well as sight. You almost instinctively think about using your zoom lens to bring a distant object closer, or about opening up and switching to a wide-angle setting to bring in more of the surrounding scenery. Think also about the conditions for good sound recording, which change just as often but more subtly. Be alert to situations that warrant switching to a more selective microphone, maybe one with a different recording pattern, to capture the scene best.

There's no dodging the fact that an additional external microphone placed at the scene of the action is the best way to get realistic sound for your videos. The external microphone connection is a handy feature to have on a camera if you plan to do some serious video work. The drawback, of course, is that the mike is attached to a cable that in turn connects to your camera. Unless you have someone to help you, you're tethered to a small area. Even a wireless mike has a maximum broadcast range of 100 feet or so. For professional results, however, an external microphone and perhaps even a separate tape recorder to collect random sounds can't be beat.

Adding Narration

Of all the sounds you'll record, the most difficult to master is narration. Good narration heightens the impact of your videos and brings the audience in closer to share in your adventures. Good ad-lib narration delivered while you're recording the scene, however, is arguably the most difficult task you'll ever undertake in shooting videos. It takes professional news reporters and sportscasters years of practice before they are able to deliver coherent, interesting, and descriptive narration for the events they cover. And remember, they're only witnessing the event and talking about it. They're not trying to make a visual record at the same time. That task is left to the camera and sound people.

So, do your own narration by all means, but practice, practice, practice until the words you want to say flow smoothly and naturally. Here are a couple of tips to help you along the way. First, turn on your TV and study the pros at work reporting sports events and quick-breaking news. They've learned how to give brief descriptions of what you see on the screen. They emphasize the little things you might miss, and they guide you into seeing the important features that help you understand what's happening.

It takes discipline to keep from talking over every scene you shoot. This is a good time to bring out those index cards you used to plan your video. Did you jot down any ideas for narration? These thoughts will be of great help to you when you begin shooting. Just check the amount of time you talk and don't chatter endlessly. The action will carry most of the story.

Remember my four-count rule for camera movement? Well, it applies to narration as well. Wait at least four seconds into the shooting before beginning your narration. Not only does this give you and your audience time to focus on the subject and to see the story unfolding, it also gives you some time and space for later editing. It's difficult for your audience to deal with a new scene jumping on the screen while at the same time a voice booms in with mindless narration. Worse still is when you don't leave yourself enough room at the beginning and the narration starts with the burp, "onald Steffens here . . . "

Only the legendary news reporter Wally Balou—the fanciful character devised by the great comedy team of Bob Elliot and Ray Goulding—could pull off this gaffe. The news reports by " . . . ly Balou at the scene of the fire . . . " were hilarious, in part because of his ineptness and bad timing. Don't be like Wally Balou. Too much happens all at once. Give the viewer a few seconds to become oriented to the sights and sounds of the new scene. Take your time before adding narration, whether you're at the scene or at the editing table. And finally, leave a cushion of at least four seconds of silence at the beginning and end of each scene.

GUIDELINES FOR GOOD COMPOSITION

There are no hard-and-fast rules for good composition in videography, but there are some basic guidelines worth considering: picture area, direction, keeping a level horizon, continuity and consistency, and the rule of thirds.

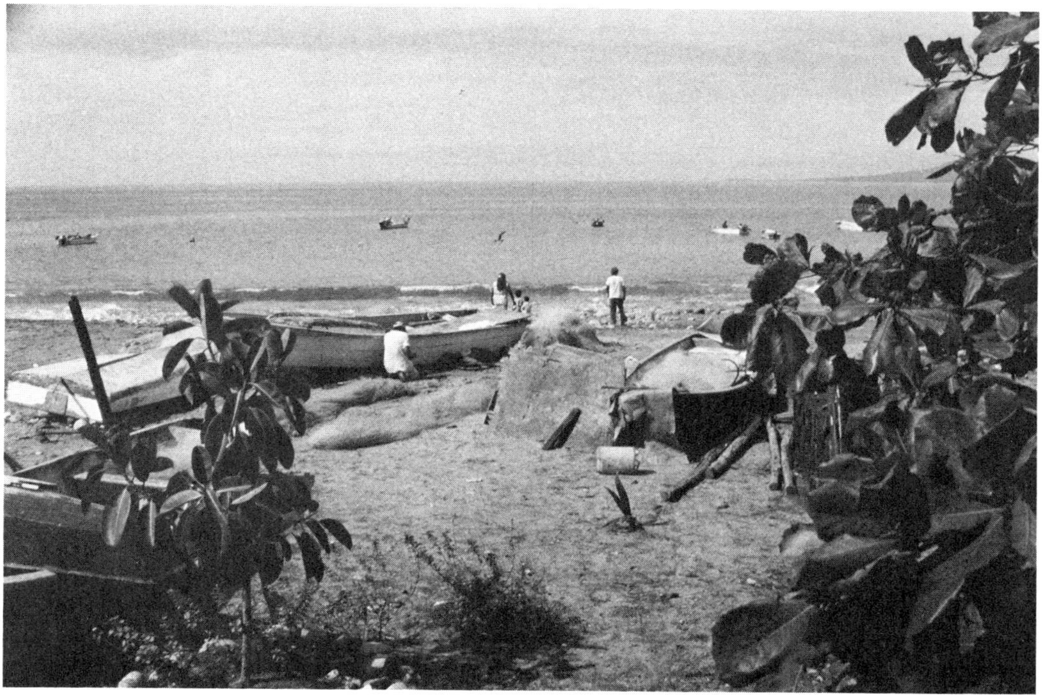

Frame your pictures for a different perspective. Even a partial frame, such as the leaves on the right, directs the viewer to the action in the background.

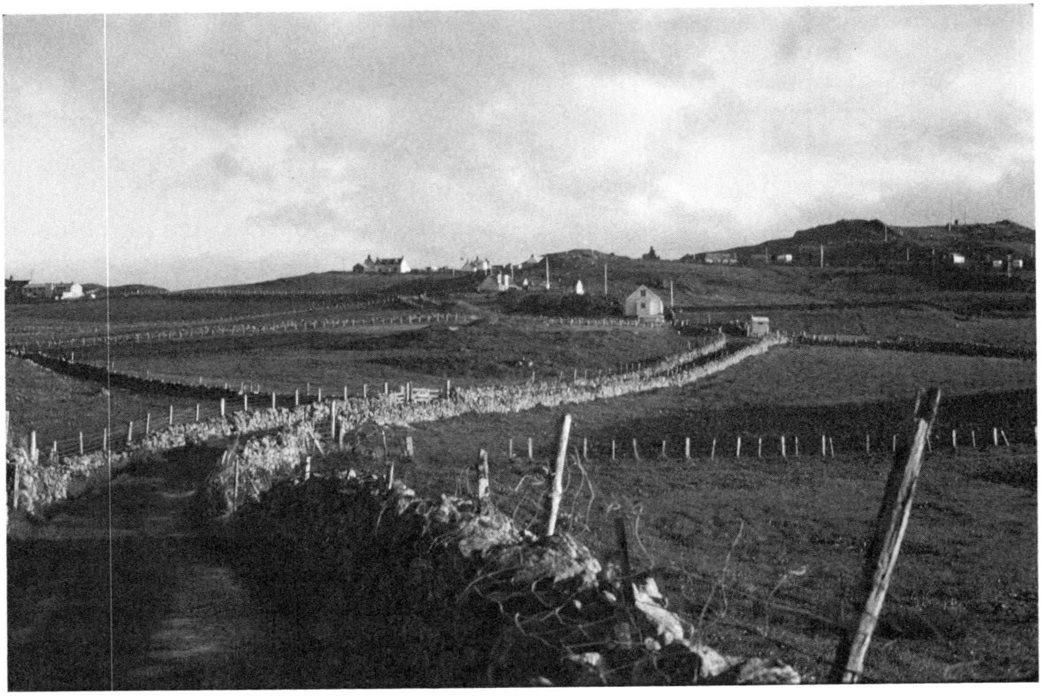

In good composition, several elements add to the harmony of a picture, including strong lines of direction. The winding road flanked by rock walls leads your eye to a little village in the background. Your next scene could be a group of people gathered in the village square. The subsequent setting in the village is a natural transition, preserving continuity. If you shoot the village scenes before the afternoon light changes or the clouds deepen, consistency of tone and color will be maintained as well.

Picture Area

Picture area refers to how much of the screen or picture is taken up with the subject itself. When taking videos of people, it's generally best to fill the screen with the subject, to get in as close as possible. I stress this because most of us are a little timid when it comes to taking pictures of other people. We don't like to intrude, and our shyness leads to those faraway shots where the emphasis seems to be on the open sky rather than on the real subjects, the people in action.

Another aspect of picture area is the idea of *framing* the scene—putting a frame or border around the picture you're shooting. This is an important element of good composition because it gives a scene depth and added interest. Framing is really a foreground border that directs your eye to the background where the real action is taking place. If the foreground frame is dark, that's an advantage because

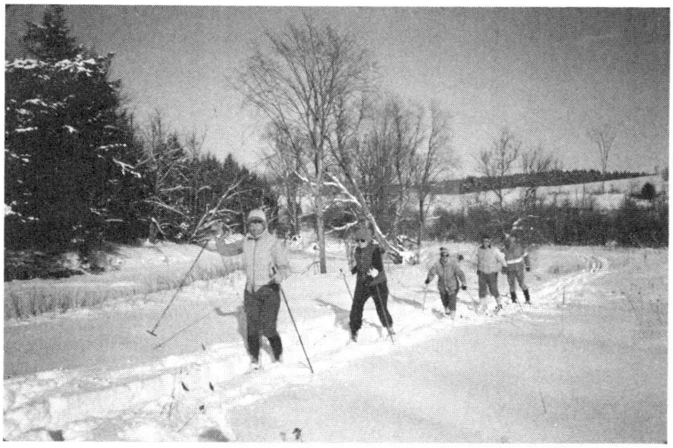

Here your eyes are directed along the line of skiers from front to back, suggesting motion. Allow the skiers to move past you and off screen. Hold that scene for a few seconds, and you've built in an automatic cutting shot to the next scene.

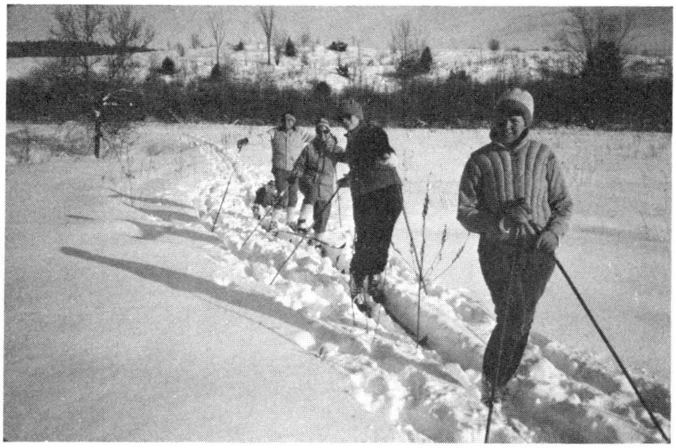

The lines of direction are good in this shot, but the continuity from the previous scene has been broken: The skiers have magically changed position, waiting to exit right, when just a moment earlier they were seen gliding off screen to the left. This break in continuity can make your audience laugh...but at the wrong time.

the main subject in the background will be naturally better lighted for greater emphasis. Trees or buildings can make effective frames because they act like a movie set to dress up the picture.

Direction

Another consideration in good composition is *direction*, which refers to lines of implied motion that move the eye toward the subject. A picket fence, for example, can lead the eye to the group of people standing at the end. Other strong lines of direction are evident in a scene along a tree-lined driveway leading to a house in the background. The placement of the trees directs your eye to the house. Or think of a wedge of football players forming to protect the ball carrier; your eye is directed to that central player, the one with the ball.

These lines of implied motion become extremely important in video because you're also working with real motion. In recording real action, you can't allow sudden changes in direction to appear on your screen. If, for example, you videotape a ball player running from left to right across the screen, your next scene should show the runner entering the picture from the left side. If the action takes place the other way around, with the player coming in from the right side, the direction is reversed and the audience is left with a confusing set of images.

Level Horizon

In virtually every outdoor scene you shoot, you'll have some sort of horizon. The horizon is that line we all perceive where the sky meets the earth. The horizon you see might not be the broad, crisp line seen at sea, where even the curvature of the earth itself is revealed. Instead, it might be a more limited one, as narrowly defined as a small section of beach or the edge of a field etched across the sky. The point is, there will be some kind of horizon, and you must remember to keep it level.

One way to do this, and it can be especially difficult on a boat, is to keep both

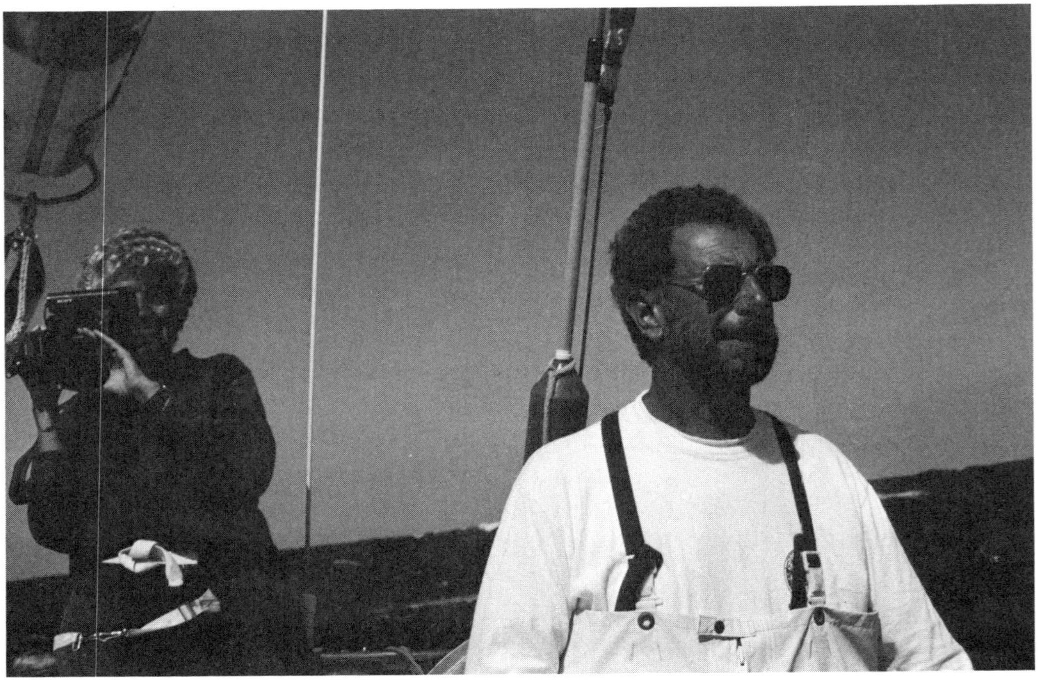

Catch the action, but don't make this mistake—keep the horizon level.

eyes open when shooting. Concentrate on one spot on the horizon, keeping it level while looking in the viewfinder. Try not to move at all. Then, let the action come to you. By having both eyes open, you see the full picture, not just what appears in the viewfinder. You can anticipate new action or elements and decide whether to include them in your next shot.

Let's use the example of a boat at sea. With both eyes open, you can see the horizon clearly, but you can also see other boats that might move into your picture. Do you want to include them? If so, record a little longer. Now you see a dock over to the right that could be confusing to your picture if you pan farther in that direction. You can end your pan early because you've seen the potential obstacle. By keeping your eyes open, you're on top of the action, and your horizon remains steady and level.

Consistency and Continuity

Our boat example leads us to a pair of words that summarize all the basic principles you need to know about video composition: consistency and continuity. They're very much alike.

Your scenes are considered *consistent* when environmental conditions match. Because of changing weather and light conditions, one scene might not match a scene shot the next day or even the next hour. Scenes shot on a sunny day simply don't match scenes shot when clouds have come in. If you don't believe me, try editing several contrasting scenes into one video sequence, and you'll see the bad results.

Continuity refers to the action of the subject and the logical flow of events. Be careful you don't allow your subjects to leave one scene only to reenter from a position that's out of context. Likewise, successive scenes in which a person's clothing keeps changing can be disturbing.

All the scenes in your video should blend together. There should be no major jumps in the continuity of a story line. Action that begins on a street corner in a city can't suddenly resume in an open field. Someone walking across a field can't, in the next scene, appear in the middle of a forest. The individual scenes need to be linked together to form a cohesive whole. Here's where cutting shots help.

We talked briefly about cutting shots earlier in this chapter. Now let's look at them in a little more detail. Cutting shots are short scenes that by themselves have little meaning and no action. When edited into the video at strategic points, however, they serve as stepping stones to the next logical scene and thus create continuity.

Think about a beach volleyball game. You begin by shooting an opening scene lasting 15 to 30 seconds of the players setting up the net and scratching out the boundary lines. If you then wait for the game to begin to start shooting again, you'll have an awkward juxtaposition of the two scenes. You need a shot to smooth the transition from one scene to the next so that the sequence has continuity. A cutting shot, lasting just a few seconds, will help bring the two scenes together. The crowd of spectators is always good for a cutting shot. Perhaps a quick view of the beach and

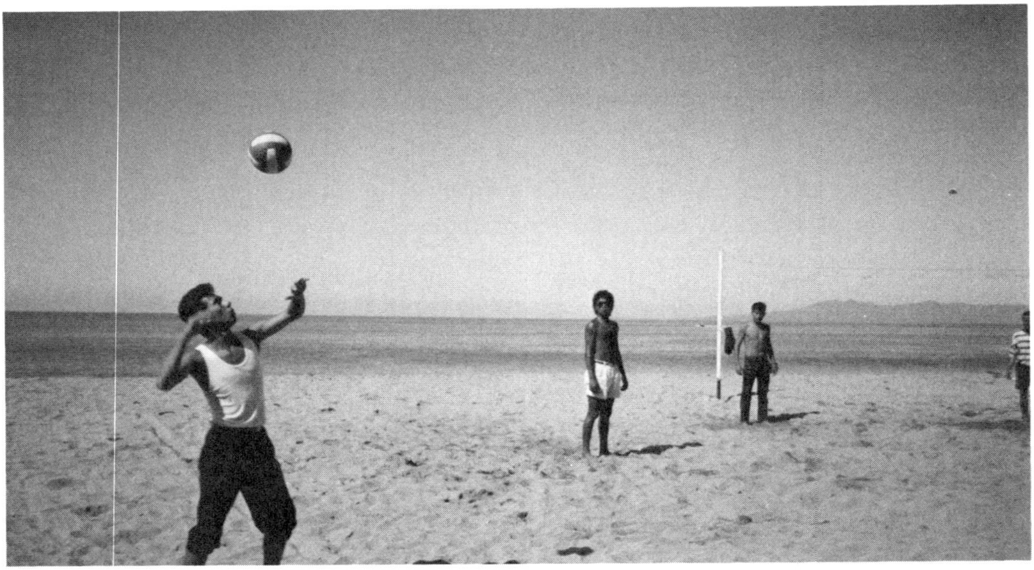

A level horizon is always important, even when the horizon is merely a background element. In this scene, the volleyball game is the main subject. Note that the sun shines at a good angle to produce pleasing shadows. The action leads naturally from the server to the team on the other side of the net.

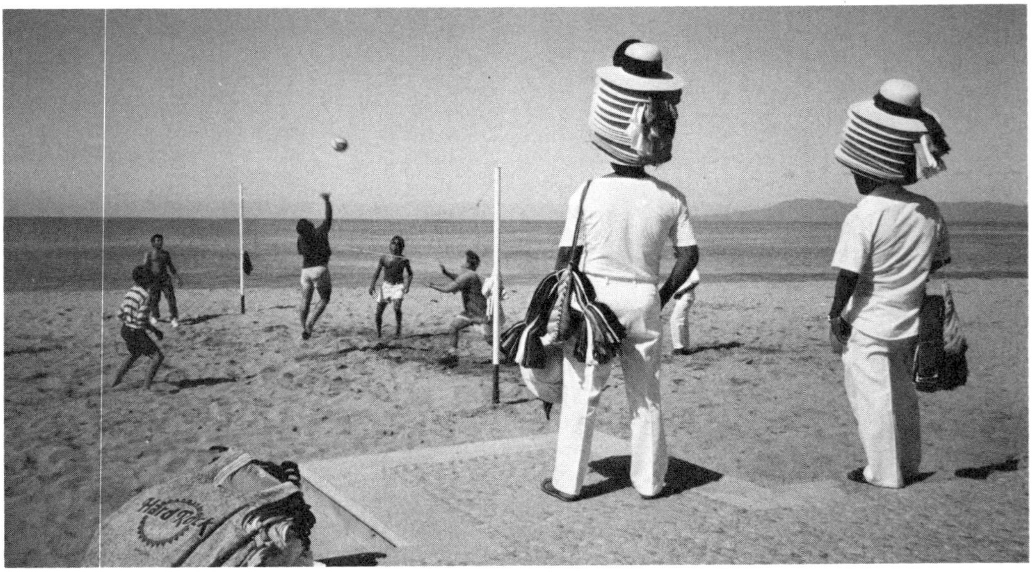

Unusual shots from the sidelines add interest to your movie. Here, souvenir salesmen pause in their rounds to watch the game.

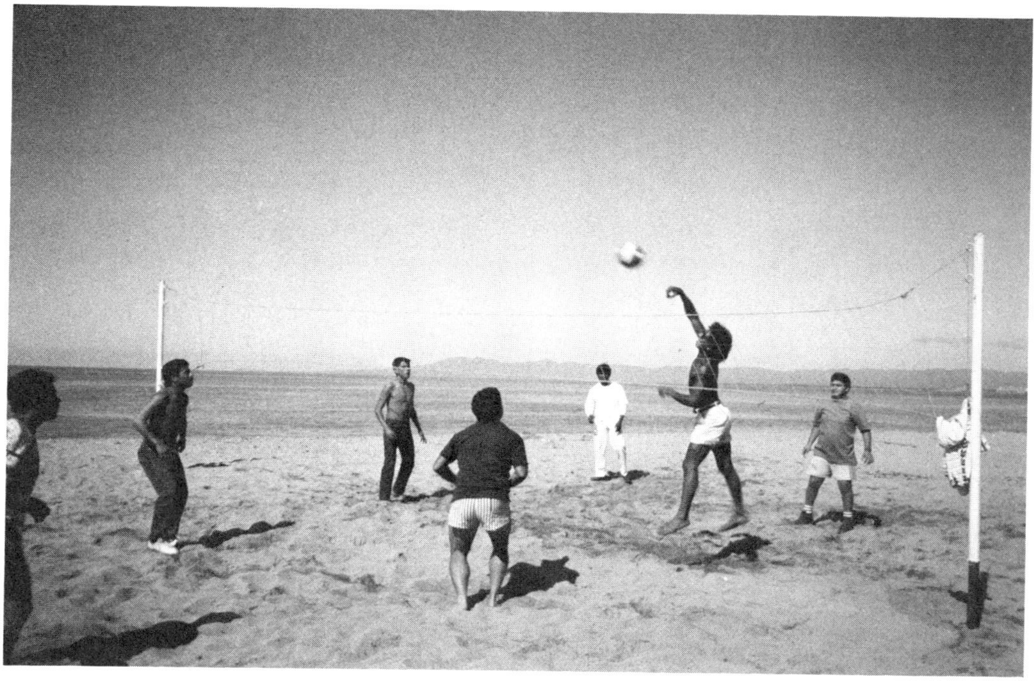

Move around to tape from different positions. Vary your close-ups with wide-angle shots, but keep one eye on maintaining a level horizon.

the water will do the trick, or even a close-up of the volleyball. Almost any static shot in the immediate area will keep the continuity of the story going.

The next time you watch a movie, pay attention to the little scenes that link the longer scenes together. Movies are filled with them. As you study this element of composition, you'll soon see similar possibilities for your own videos.

The Rule of Thirds

The *rule of thirds* comes to us from an ancient Greek philosopher who observed that dividing elements into thirds creates harmony and pleasing proportions. It works in architecture and art, and it works in videography. Like the other rules in this chapter, you needn't follow this rule absolutely, just keep it in mind when things get confused. The idea is to divide a picture into thirds either vertically or horizontally, depending on how you're framing the picture. The rule is most easily applied to still photography, but it has some good applications in videos as well. It's just a little harder to keep moving subjects in their proper places when shooting action videos.

Beach and water scenes offer the best examples of how to use the rule of thirds horizontally. Reduced to simple terms, most beach scenes are dominated by three

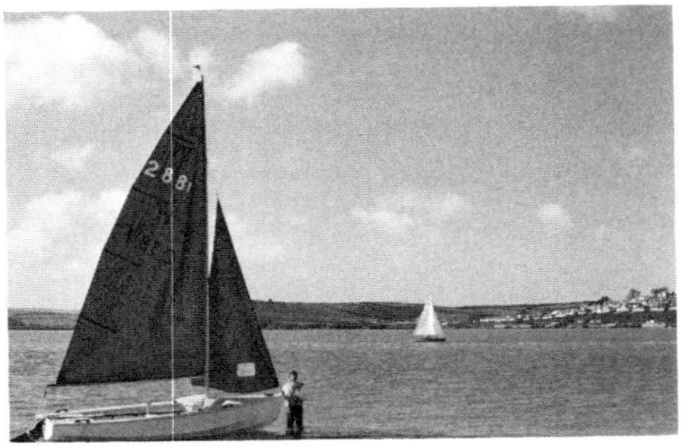

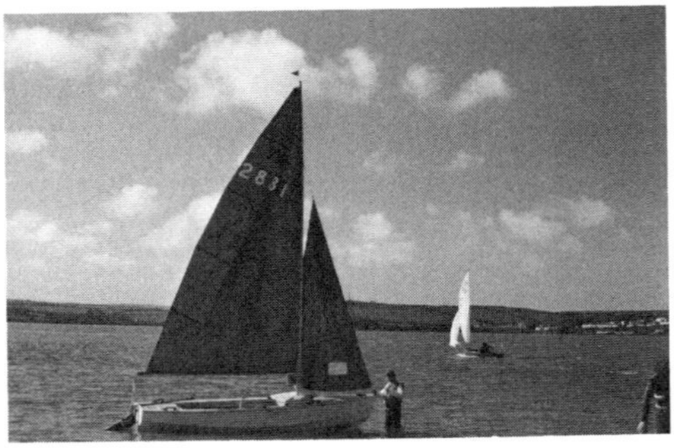

The rule of thirds is broken in the picture on the left, yet the weight of the sailboat is somewhat balanced by the other boat and structures on the right. Is this better or worse than the similar photograph that follows? As the videographer, you decide where the emphasis should be. There are no hard-and-fast rules when it comes to good composition.

horizontal lines of attention: the land, the sea, and the sky. Regardless of what else might be in the picture, each of these lines attracts attention. It's generally best to have the land occupy the bottom third of the picture; the water, the middle third; and the sky, the top third. The resulting picture will be balanced and comfortable to look at. If you were to allow the land to fill two-thirds of the picture, the squeezed-in sea and sky would look out of place and distorted. Worse still would be an omission of the sky entirely with just a broad patch of sand and the endless sea reaching up and out of the picture.

Remember to consider vertical thirds as well. Here, too, dividing the picture into thirds helps develop pleasing composition and balance. Avoid placing one main object—a person, a building, or anything else—squarely in the middle of your picture. Think about thirds and place your subject off to one side, balanced by something else on the opposite side. In our beach example, a nicely balanced and interesting shot might consist of a man, a woman, and a child occupying the left side of the picture, extending toward the middle. Their attention is directed to the right, where the beach line ends and the water reaches out to the horizon. Near the horizon a sailboat is moving along the coastline, traveling from right to left. The overall picture is pleasing.

The scene also illustrates some other points of good composition related to the rule of thirds. The family group on the left fills a large portion of the picture area. As they gaze out to sea, they point to the boat, directing the viewers' eyes to the right. The boat has entered the picture from the right and has plenty of room to move left. We are comfortably contained in this picture. Now allow the natural action to take place. Let the boat sail to the left while the people on shore follow it with their own movements. The result is a nicely structured scene, all because you followed the guidelines of good composition.

CHAPTER FOUR

Shooting in the Four Seasons

Shooting videos outdoors can present some major challenges to professionals and amateurs alike. Humidity, dust, and glare can all wreak havoc on delicate electronic devices. Learning how to deal with these hazards will make your outings more enjoyable and your videos more successful. This chapter offers advice on how to contend with the worst nature has to offer, and discusses the techniques, equipment, and methodology used in winter videos, warm-weather videos, underwater videos, and wildlife videos.

COPING WITH THE ELEMENTS

The outdoor videographer faces problems not found indoors, and especially not in the studio—problems dictated by the elements themselves: glare, salt and sand, dirt and dust, temperature extremes, and wind noise.

Glare

Light, of course, is a prime requirement for videos. Without sufficient light, you can't record images. Too much light, however, can be just as big a problem. Excessive light bouncing into the camera lens is glare, which can ruin not only your videos, but the sensitive electronic components in your camera as well.

Glare comes from the direct rays of the sun or from the reflection of the sun's light off a shiny surface. Snow, sand, and water all reflect light and can produce glare. So whether you're shooting at the beach, on the water, or on the ski slopes, you must be aware of the problems associated with glare. If you have to squint, there's glare. If you're wearing sunglasses because it's too bright, there's probably glare.

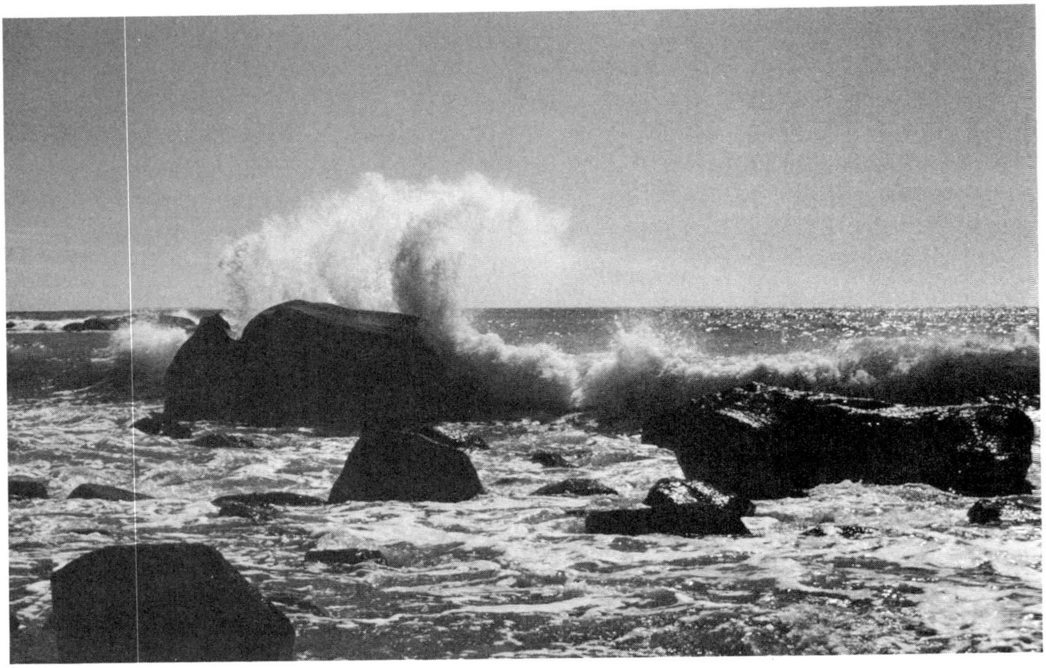

Let the action come to you. Beware of glare, though, since it can affect delicate camera sensors and give incorrect light-intensity readings.

The easiest way to avoid glare is to shoot your videos with the sun at a 45-degree angle behind you, shining over one shoulder. It's not always possible, but at least try to keep the sun behind you. Anytime the sun is directly overhead or in front of you, you run the risk of glare and reflection.

When glare is unavoidable, consider using one of the neutral-density filters introduced in Chapter 2. A neutral-density filter cuts down on glare by reducing the light in your picture. Look in the viewfinder to see if adding the filter does the job. If it doesn't, try the polarizing filter, which eliminates glare and gives new richness to the colors around you. Remember, though, that using a polarizing filter, or any filter for that matter, adds another dimension to your video that must be accounted for. In scenes shot with the filter in place, the sky and other elements in the picture will have different color qualities than scenes shot without the filter—an obvious break in consistency. Only a totally different scene shot next in sequence or edited in later will enable you to get away with these tonal differences. Sometimes a cutting shot will provide the visual distance needed to go on to a scene shot without the filter.

Salt and Sand

Be extra careful when you take your video camera to the beach or out in a boat in salt water. Salt and sand are formidable opponents with millions of years' experience in wrecking man's best tools. Saltwater spray is a compound problem because it's highly corrosive and the salt crystals themselves are abrasive. Sand is deadly on cameras and other fragile devices. It's like tiny ground-up particles of glass that seem able to penetrate almost anything. It's not a good idea to wipe the sand away because you risk grinding in the particles, making the situation worse. Instead, carry a can of compressed air in a separate bag to blow away the salt or sand particles without rubbing.

Here's a tip I picked up from a serious beach-goer, not a professional photographer. This man often traveled with his family to the seashore in the summer and enjoyed taking his video camera along. To guard against excessive heat and humidity at the beach, he kept the camera in a medium-sized foam picnic cooler with a couple of silica-gel packs that he picked up for free at a local photography store. The clerk at the store had dozens of the desiccant packages left over from camera lens shipments and was happy to give a few away.

My friend also used the cooler as a traveling case for his video equipment, and reported that it was particularly effective for storage in his car, where summertime temperatures often reached over 90 degrees Fahrenheit. He didn't keep ice or cold beer in it, of course, just the camera and the gel packs. It worked wonderfully. In addition, if he went swimming, he worried less that someone would steal his camera, as it was cleverly disguised as his lunch.

Dirt and Dust

Dirt and dust bring their own problems to video equipment, but these are more easily remedied. Clean the exterior parts of your camera periodically with a water-dampened cloth or a clean cotton swab. Avoid using chemical solutions for the plastic housing and rubber parts of the camera since they can be damaged by cleaning agents such as ammonia and alcohol. Some chemicals actually dissolve plastic, so it's best to stay away from most modern cleaners and stick to soft, lint-free cloths dampened with water. Linen is lovely, and gentlemen's handkerchiefs used to be made of the finest linen. Find a gentleman, if you can, and ask him if he'll give you his clean handkerchief. It will make a great camera accessory.

Temperature Extremes

Next in this short list of natural hazards is temperature extremes. Anyone who has taken pictures outdoors with a still camera knows the problems inherent in sudden temperature changes, the biggest of which is condensation. Moisture condensing around the camera lens or operating controls can penetrate the camera and eventually corrode the delicate electrical components. Moisture is a problem everywhere, even in hot, dry climates. Rain is clearly a threat to any electronic instrument, but fog and mist also bring trouble as moisture collects on delicate controls.

Your camera probably has a moisture sensor built into the electronic circuitry. When the moisture level in the camera gets too high, a tiny LED (light-emitting diode) glows in the viewfinder to let you know there's a problem, and the camera temporarily reverts to standby mode. Usually, if you wait a short time with the camera on but not running, the unit heats up sufficiently to dry the moisture, the light goes out, and you can resume shooting. Video cameras like a little warmth to operate properly, but they don't work well with rapidly fluctuating temperatures.

In winter, condensation leads to freezing, which can ruin any piece of electronic equipment. Tiny droplets of water can penetrate the camera housing or lens fitting and then freeze the parts inside. One of the most vulnerable areas is the tape transport deck where you load the tape into the camera. This opening leads directly to all the mechanical workings of the camera—the wheels and gears that move the tape across the recording and playback heads. Keep this area bone-dry, if possible. If it gets damp, carefully dry it with a drop of isopropyl alcohol on a foam applicator or a cotton swab. This gentle alcohol treatment also cleans the recording and playback heads at the same time.

People commonly keep their cameras under their parkas for protection from the snow and cold. This offers only false security. When you bring the camera out into the open, warmed now by the heat of your body, condensation will form as the camera hits the cold outside air. If that happens, dry off the camera as soon as possible with a clean cloth.

Condensation doesn't occur when your equipment maintains a constant temperature, either warm or cold. Think about keeping your camera where temperature fluctuations are minimized. It's generally better to have your camera stay cold rather than be subjected to extremes. Don't be overly protective when you're out in the open. Guard your equipment from being banged about and from getting wet, but also know that it's certainly sturdy enough to be in the open rather than kept tightly under wraps and then exposed to harsh conditions.

Clean with caution

Please be extremely careful when cleaning the inside of your camera. Cotton swabs must be used with care because loose strands of cotton can get caught in the delicate mechanisms and cause problems. Be extra cautious when cleaning the recording and playback heads; they're very sensitive to pressure and abrasion. Just brush across them lightly from side to side with a swab dampened with alcohol. Don't clean them with a vertical motion. Keep the alcohol away from all plastic parts, including the camera housing, and use it sparingly only on the inside transport machinery. Proper cleaning of your equipment in all seasons prolongs its working life and gives you many years of good service.

Occasionally, you'll find moisture developing inside the lens. This usually evaporates without causing any real damage. If the condition persists, take your camera and lens to a professional repair center for cleaning and servicing. It's not a bad idea to do this on a regular basis, say once a year. Keep your camera dry and protected from the elements until you want to use it. Then, handle it with care and clean the housing and lens surface after each use. That way, you give it the best chance to survive and to serve you for many years—or at least until you decide to upgrade to a newer and better model.

Rain coats for protection

Adverse weather conditions sometimes call for the use of protective covers for your video equipment. These "rain coats" are constructed of heavy-duty plastic with a reinforced window (sometimes made of glass) for the camera lens. They're not specifically waterproof and can't be used for underwater videography, but these protective housings will keep rain and snow away from your valuable equipment and still allow you to shoot your video.

Some covers are designed to encase the camera completely, forcing you to grope through the plastic covering to work the controls. At first this feels like typing on a computer keyboard while wearing mittens, but you quickly get used to the new feeling and soon learn to operate the controls with little trouble. The most versatile coverings are open at the bottom or can be sealed with a strip of Velcro. This is more like slipping a plastic bag over the camera: it doesn't protect the camera as well, but it enables you to operate the controls directly. Regardless of manufacturers' claims, you lose some measure of clarity with these devices because you're shooting through another lens. The loss is small, though, and will probably go unnoticed when compared to unprotected videos shot in the rain or misty fog. Some type of protective cover is an accessory worth looking at, especially if you're planning to shoot in inclement weather or in places where salt, sand, or snow predominate.

Be aware that although these covers protect your camera from the rain and mist, they don't protect it from condensation. Condensation is always a problem whenever temperatures change or ventilation is inadequate.

Wind Noise

The problem with wind is twofold: it kicks up tiny particles of dust and debris, and it produces noise. Even a wind sock (foam padding covering the microphone) doesn't stop the microphone from picking up and amplifying the sound of the blowing wind. You can cover the microphone with even more padding, but this further muffles the sounds you want. Experiment with additional wind protection until you find a balance that allows for some wind background noise while permitting normal speaking voices to be heard clearly. Sony recently introduced a series of palmcorders that can sense excessive wind noise and effectively remove it.

Whenever possible, shoot your videos downwind. Keeping your back to the wind cuts down on extraneous wind noise. If one position doesn't work, look for another that might better protect the sound you want on your video. You might consider removing the microphone temporarily. This choice courts the problem of a "reality gap," to be sure, but you'll have complete control of the sound. With practice, you can add the right sounds at the right levels during postproduction editing.

THE WINTER VIDEO

The biggest challenge in making winter videos, aside from protecting the camera from freezing, is getting good light. In northern regions, the winter sun is a pale cousin to the fiery disk we see in the summer or in the tropics. The sun's rays are often diffused through a layer of clouds, so the available light can be flat, shadowless, and cold. It's difficult to videotape under such conditions because there's little or no contrast. When the sun does come out from behind the clouds, however, it illuminates your winter videos nicely. Since the sun is actually in the southern sky in the winter, and is lower on the horizon than it is in the summer, its rays strike the earth at a more oblique angle. This is good because there's little risk of unfavorable noontime shadows from the sun shining directly overhead. Another advantage is that almost any shot in any direction (except directly south) will be illuminated nicely with the sun off to one side.

The real concern in shooting winter videos comes from glare and the reflected light off an icy or snowy background. The camera's sensors are affected by the white background and the great contrasts inherent in winter scenes. This is when you'll need to adjust the aperture setting manually. If you allow the camera to set the aperture automatically, the light sensors will be forever adjusting and readjusting to the changing light values, causing annoying flares and quick blackouts. The sensors will close the aperture to account for the bright background, leaving your subject literally in the dark. To capture your subject in the proper light, you need to use a wider aperture to achieve more exposure.

Another solution to winter's glare is to use a filter, just as you would in the summer when shooting scenes at the beach. If the skylight filter doesn't sufficiently cut the glare, try one of the neutral-density filters.

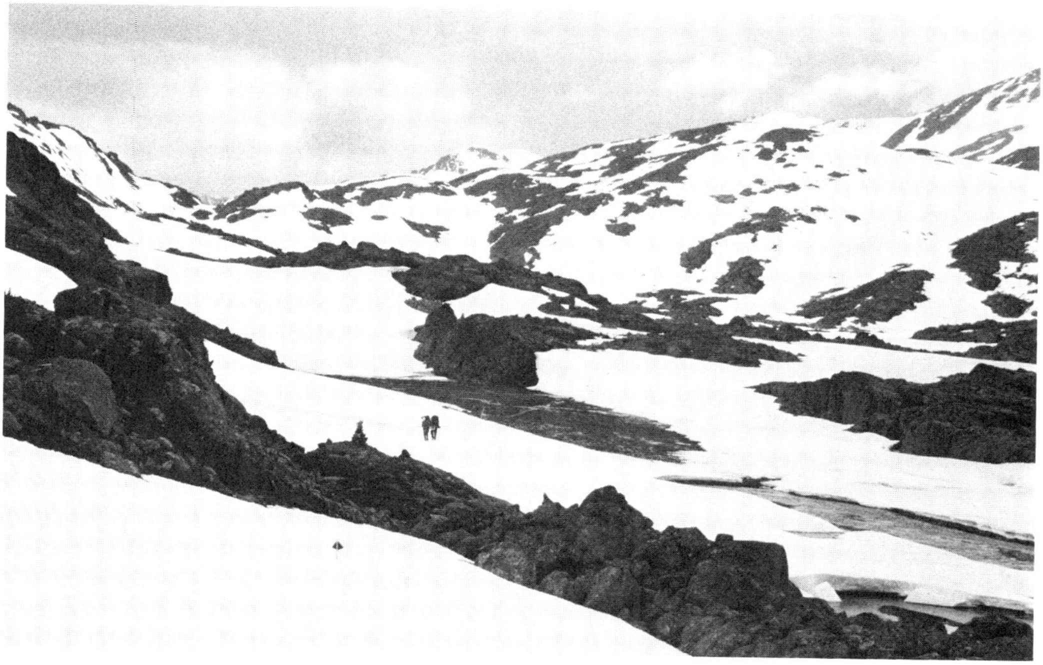

Snow and ice as background elements present special problems for automatic sensors, forcing the aperture to close. Here you would take your exposure readings manually off the rock outcroppings to ensure balanced exposure of the people in the center. Start with a tight close-up—a telephoto shot—of the hikers and then zoom out to reveal the full panorama.

The Vertical Touch

In Chapter 3 we talked about the importance of keeping the horizon level. At the beach, this is easy because the horizon is clearly visible. On the ski slopes, however, the horizon is often hidden behind the tree line, making it harder for you to keep things level. It's easy to become confused by the "apparent" horizon, the angled mountainside in front of you. The difficulty is in keeping the correct pitch, neither exaggerating nor flattening the slope. The best way to do this is to let the trees be your guide. Trees grow straight up. Instead of concentrating on keeping the horizon horizontal, concentrate instead on keeping the trees vertical. Your videos will be straight and true.

This is extremely important in shooting videos of Alpine skiing, because the angle of the slope is what gives your scenes drama and impact. The perspective is best when you shoot across the slope rather than directly at it or down on it from high up on the chairlift. The trees growing straight up provide a nice contrast with the pitch of the hill. Above the tree line, Alpine skiing takes on a different character with broad, open slopes. The perspective here is emphasized by shooting against the sky, with mountain peaks forming the backdrop. This is where zooming out from a close-up of a skier to a wide-angle shot of the grand panorama can be so effective.

Keep the Action Coming Your Way

When shooting sports videos in the winter (or in any other season, for that matter) it's always best to let the action come to you. Your scenes will have more life and vitality if the action comes toward the camera rather than you trying to follow it from behind. Position yourself so that skiers or skaters are heading your way. You can always follow the action with a panning shot (remember the four-count rule), and then let the action flow naturally out of the picture. This gives you an open scene so that you can introduce new material in the next scene. It's really a simple editing technique done with the camera, and it gives you great flexibility for the scenes to follow.

Planning Your Day on the Slopes

When planning your video of a day on the slopes, think of the natural sequence of events. The skiers put on their skis and boots in one area, usually the base lodge. The lift attendants guide the skiers to the chairlift that takes them to the summit. Other attendants assist them at the top, where they gather in preparation for the downhill run. They usually ski relatively short sections at a time, stopping frequently before setting off on a new part of the trail. If you stop to examine the activity more carefully, you'll see that you can plan a simple story line and then shoot the scenes in a logical sequence that will easily play back in finished form. Opportunities abound at ski resorts for great scenes, including the short cutting shots you need to tie the big scenes together.

Covering Nordic skiing events is much the same as covering Alpine events, with just a few differences. The cold and the glare are the same, and the motion is similar, but cross-country skiers move more slowly and sedately. You still need to keep the horizon level, but it's much easier with the flatter terrain. Those essential cutting shots might be a little more difficult to find because you're in a more natural setting, but the opportunities are still there.

Ski jumping, the other half of Nordic skiing, is more of a spectacle sport that takes place in a unique setting. These skiers race down a high ramp and then launch themselves into the air to soar high above the spectators gathered below. The pageantry surrounding ski jumping is obvious and easy to shoot: jumpers waiting their turns at the summit, making last-minute adjustments to their bindings, checking the running surfaces of their skis, testing the winds; the crowd gathered below; more people standing along the steep slopes leading from the jump. The real test comes when the jumper streaks down the track and launches into the air.

Make no mistake, this is a tough, quick shot, and you have to deal with the overall brightness of the sky, the relatively small solitary jumper, the speed of flight, the contrasting light values coming from the snow, the crowd of people, the trees in the background, and probably more. But this is not an impossible task. If you think about it, you've already shot videos of skiers on a steep downhill run. You've seen birds flying overhead against a bright sky. The water skier at the lake last summer made several good jumps off an anchored ramp in the center of the lake. The beach scenes you shot showed good contrast between sand and surf, and you minimized glare by shooting away from the direct rays of the sun. Your cutting shots of people standing in a reception line for an outdoor wedding gave extra life to another video you made. Now, at the site of this ski-jumping exhibition, all the lessons learned from past experiences should come together. You might even get the feeling you've done it all before . . . and, in fact, you have.

WARM-WEATHER VIDEOS

All the lessons you learned about shooting winter sports can be applied directly to any warm-weather videos you might want to make about hiking or running. We've changed seasons, to be sure, and you don't have to be concerned with freezing temperatures and snow reflections. But while the settings have changed and the sunlight is different, the movements of the people in your video are familiar. You have a good idea of how they're going to move and approximately where they'll end up. Getting into position to record sprinters lunging to the finish line is really not much different from finding the right spot to videotape the winner of a ski race. The techniques you used when videotaping cross-country skiers gliding across a snowy field are the same ones you'll use to record hikers or runners or even a group of kids playing in the backyard.

Take your video camera to the beach in summer or to the tropics on a winter holiday, and you'll find many similar situations with just a few new challenges. The temperature of the air is certainly different, the humidity is high, and the blowing sand and salt spray is in the air. But when reduced to basic elements, you've encountered them before. It's still important to keep your equipment at an even temperature, away from humidity, and out of harm's way. The sun is higher in the sky, but the glare off the water is like the light reflected off ice, and the sandy beach even reflects the light of the sun just as the snow does. The horizon line between sea and sky is much stronger and more evident here than it is in many other outdoor shots, though, so you have to work harder to keep it level. If the horizon is even a little tilted, it will be disturbing to your audience.

And so it goes from one venue to the next, and from one activity to another. Use the experiences learned in one video shoot to your advantage in the next by remembering what they have in common.

UNDERWATER VIDEOS

We can't look at outdoor videos, especially those shot around the water or at the beach, without some mention of videos shot under the water. Underwater videography, even if it's only of short duration in shallow water, is complex but exciting because you're on the edge of a new frontier.

When considering underwater videography, be aware that you're entering a different world, a potentially dangerous world where specialized training and equipment are necessary. The first requirement for underwater work is proper water safety training, and the best is scuba certification for open-water diving. (Scuba is an acronym for self-contained underwater breathing apparatus.) Even if you plan only shallow dives with snorkel mask and tube, a scuba course will help you develop the skills you need to operate safely and confidently in the water.

There are many devices on the market for this sport. The first one you need to consider is a waterproof camera housing or a video camera specially designed for underwater use (Sony recently introduced a moderately priced underwater camera). Your underwater shots don't have to be complicated, and it's certainly not mandatory that you have all the most sophisticated underwater equipment being developed. You can shoot effective videos using even the most rudimentary equipment, such as a glass-bottom bucket that enables you to shoot in shallow water just below the surface. A simple tool such as this is available in most hardware or general-merchandise stores anywhere in the tropics. They're popular among reef fishermen and people who like to peer down into the water without getting wet.

If deeper water intrigues you, or if you want more than a bird's-eye view, here are a few tips from David Doubillet, chief underwater photographer for the National Geographic Society. His startling underwater photographs have appeared in countless publications of the Society, including *National Geographic* magazine. David works primarily with photographic film, but his techniques and tips apply to videotape as well.

First of all, David never dives alone. He can't. He needs additional divers to help set up special underwater lights and secondary cameras, and to arrange for emergency procedures or support boats. You won't have to worry too much about burdensome equipment, but it's still safer not to dive alone. The "buddy system" of having someone dive with you is a key tenet of scuba training. Having another pair of human eyes down there is also helpful in pointing out delights as well as possible dangers.

If you're already a practiced diver, but are interested in adding videography to your dives, be aware that you're adding a layer of complication. In addition to the weight and bulk of the scuba equipment (including compressed air tanks, neutral buoyancy vests, weight belts, and breathing regulators), you have to add the camera gear, protective camera housings, special waterproof lights, and large battery packs. This stuff is heavy and extremely awkward to lug about. It's all much more complex than shooting on land.

Using supplementary lighting is also more difficult than it is on dry land. The emphasis underwater is not on subtle lighting, but rather on pure illumination. It's best to have multiple lights instead of a basic single light. Several lights give depth to a scene, which otherwise would seem like a black hole with only a small, central image illuminated. Arranging those extra lights, however, is not something you can do alone. This is when a partner can help; just remember that you have to be able to communicate with him or her without being able to yell, "Hey, turn the light a little this way!"

Another problem underwater involves viewing your subject. On land, you simply place the camera to your eye and shoot. Underwater, there's distortion and distance. The viewing distance from your eye through the glass of the face mask through the waterproof housing to the viewfinder is several inches. Consequently, regular viewfinders are useless underwater. The solution is to have a frame sight constructed on the camera. This is a bit like the World War I airplane gun sight that was used before the development of good optics. It's primitive and serves only to point the way. The frame site, made of plastic or metal, is mounted above the camera so that you can line up the subject and shoot.

The refraction of light (the bending of light waves) by water is another major consideration when shooting underwater. Because of light refraction, objects underwater appear closer and larger than they really are. A good rule of thumb is that 12 inches correlates to only 9 inches underwater due to refraction. So, set the focus at three-quarters the actual distance. Automatic focusing generally makes the correction, but this is a handy formula to remember, especially when you can't get close enough to the viewfinder to check whether objects are in focus.

Unless there's a special need for a close-up shot that would require the macro setting, or unless you have very good specialty lenses for underwater work, it's best to keep your lens at a wide-angle setting. The wide-angle setting generally allows for a wider aperture setting so as to gather more light, always a good thing underwater. In addition, a wide-angle setting reveals more of the immediate underwater area. Remember, you can't control where a fish goes, so the wider the field you encompass, the more chance you'll have of keeping your subject in view. A large brain coral will stay still, but not a school of fish. It's hard to get fish to hold still for "just one more."

You also have the limitation of bottom time when shooting underwater videos. If you're just ducking under the surface with mask and snorkel, your time is limited by how long you can hold your breath. If you're a certified scuba diver, your underwater time is still measured only in minutes, and the deeper you go, the shorter the time you have. Whatever you hope to shoot has to be planned within the limits of the dive itself. A good dive plan is very much like a good video shooting plan. Both are necessary in this kind of activity.

The late great baseball legend Satchel Page had some rules for living that he liked to share with almost everyone he met. One of his sayings was, "As you go through life, don't ever look back 'cause something might be gaining on you." Underwater, that's probably the best reason there is to look back. If you're interested in a school of little fish, something else might be as well. Big fish eat little fish. If you see something large becoming interested in you, leave the area slowly, but with strength and confidence. Don't make any sudden or threatening moves. Just ease on out. No fish really wants to take on something very strange and possibly troublesome, which you represent with all your gear and equipment. Just don't decide to challenge the resident landlord. It might make good footage, but it's better to be able to return another day.

WILDLIFE VIDEOS

You need two things to take good wildlife videos: a long lens and plenty of patience. It's a big challenge, and all the lessons you learned earlier in technique and composition come into play, including all the cautions about weather and difficult light conditions. Add to it the unpredictable movements and reactions of the animals and birds, and you have the ingredients of a most demanding pursuit. But while the challenges might be great, the rewards of a successful wildlife video certainly justify the effort.

It's not necessary to embark on an African safari or even a pack-mule exploration in the Rocky Mountains to get good wildlife videos. For a start, you might consider the birds and beasts in your own backyard. For most of us, those critters are at least familiar, if not actually friendly. But if more exotic animals excite you, go first to a zoo or park preserve where the animals are displayed in various levels of confinement. A zoo is a wonderful place to go on your video safari because in one short afternoon, you can be magically transported to all the remote corners of the world where wild, ferocious animals still roam and exotic birds fly overhead.

You'll need a good telephoto lens to catch your subjects on videotape, so plan to spend some extra time and money with your video equipment dealer. The standard zoom lens you get with your video camera might work for the animals in small cages, but if you're going any further afield, the off-the-shelf model just won't do the job you have in mind. There are specialty lenses for the extreme telephoto needs of wildlife videos, and there are video cameras with the ability to accept these interchangeable lenses. As of this writing, these are not widely marketed, however, and

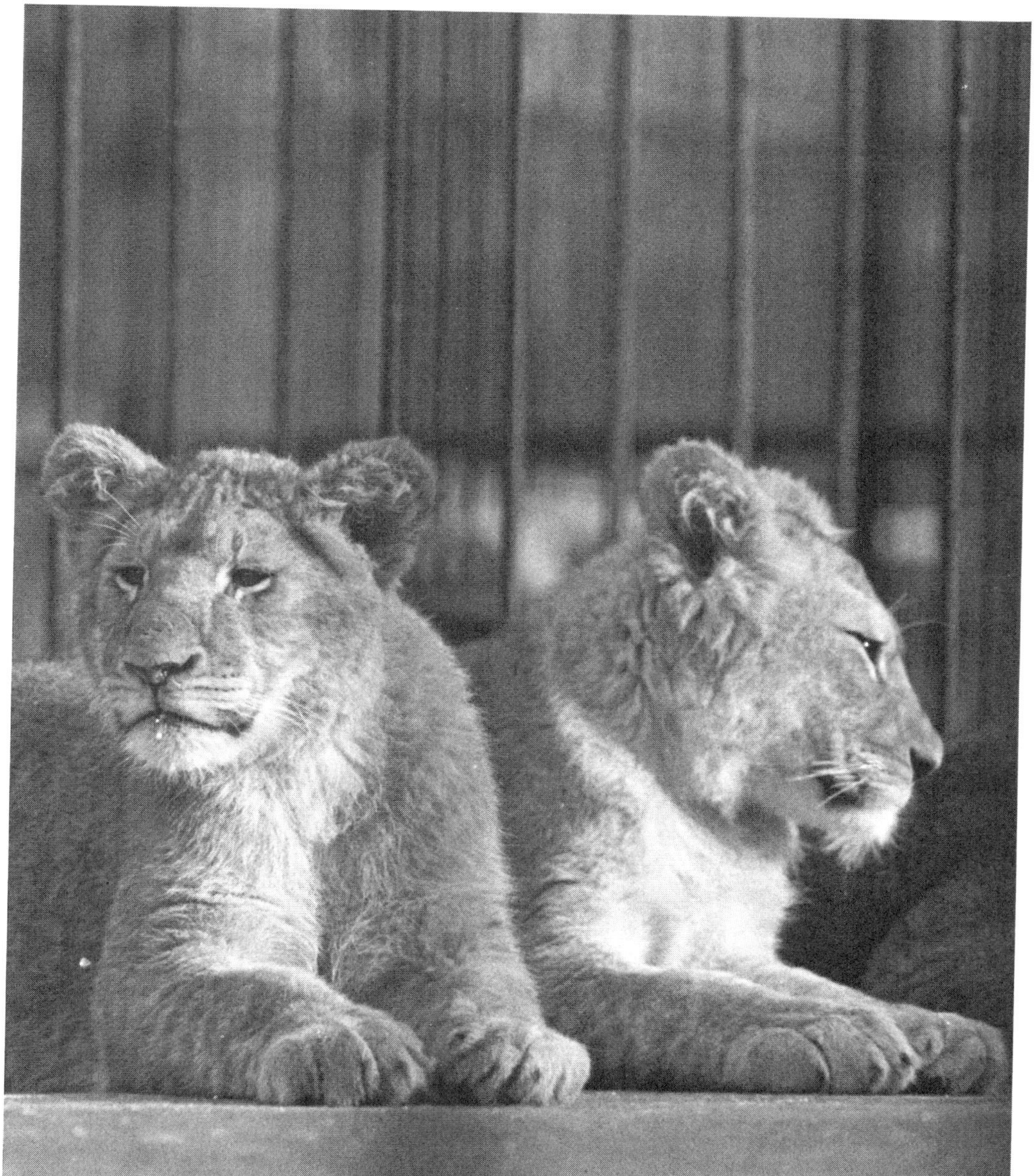

Manual focusing enables you to alter the depth of field and blur the background and zero-in on the subject. With the lens positioned between the bars, you can barely see that these lions are in a cage. Since they're relatively still and the light is even, with no bright highlights or areas of deep shadow, automatic shutter speed and automatic aperture settings are best here.

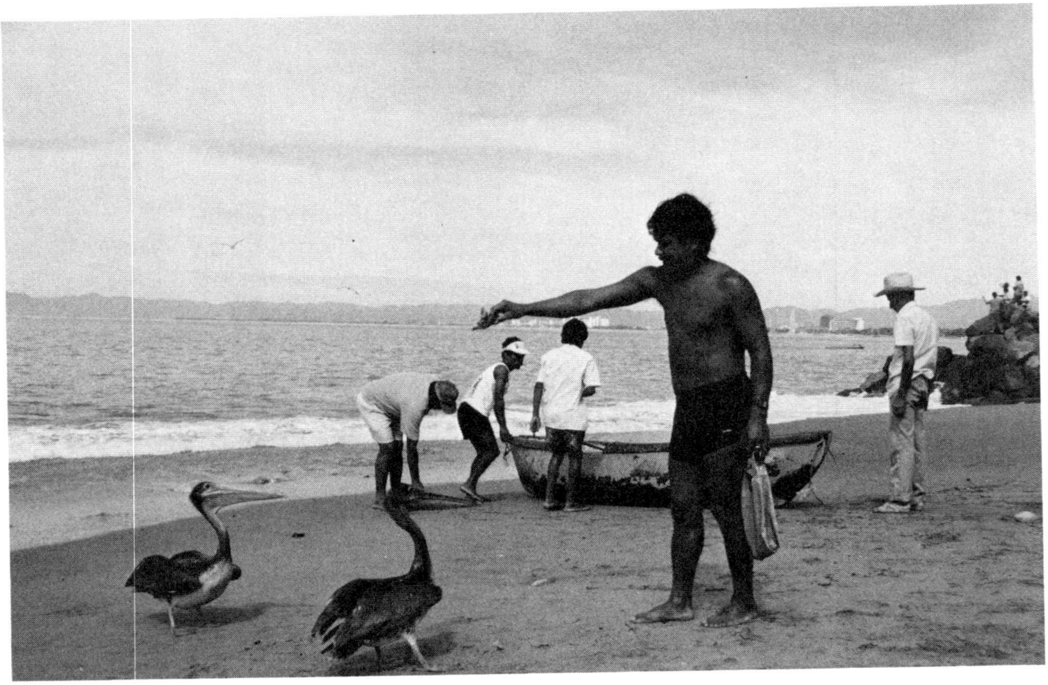

Common birds are sometimes more photogenic than unusual birds. A shot of a pelican walking along or being hand-fed by a passer-by would make a good cutting shot in a video about a day at the beach.

the cost is high. An alternative is a telephoto lens extender you add to your zoom lens (see Chapter 2), thus increasing the power fourfold or more, albeit with a small loss of picture quality.

In the zoo, you'll probably be within range of most of the game and can shoot video between the bars of most outdoor cages. It seems almost too obvious to say, but people make foolish mistakes everyday. Please be careful not to get within grabbing range of wild animals. Lions, tigers, and bears are notoriously untrustworthy around humans, and their razor-clawed reach is surprisingly long and swift. Don't tempt them and, above all, don't taunt them.

With a little effort and imagination, you can get close enough to zoo animals to get some marvelous shots. If the bars do get in your way, you can shoot through them by using the manual controls for distance and aperture. By extending the lens to infinity and opening the aperture as wide as possible, you effectively reduce the depth of field to include just the subject you focus on. Objects close at hand, in this case the bars of the animal's cage, will be so out of focus they almost disappear. At worst, they'll appear as faint blurs on each side of the picture.

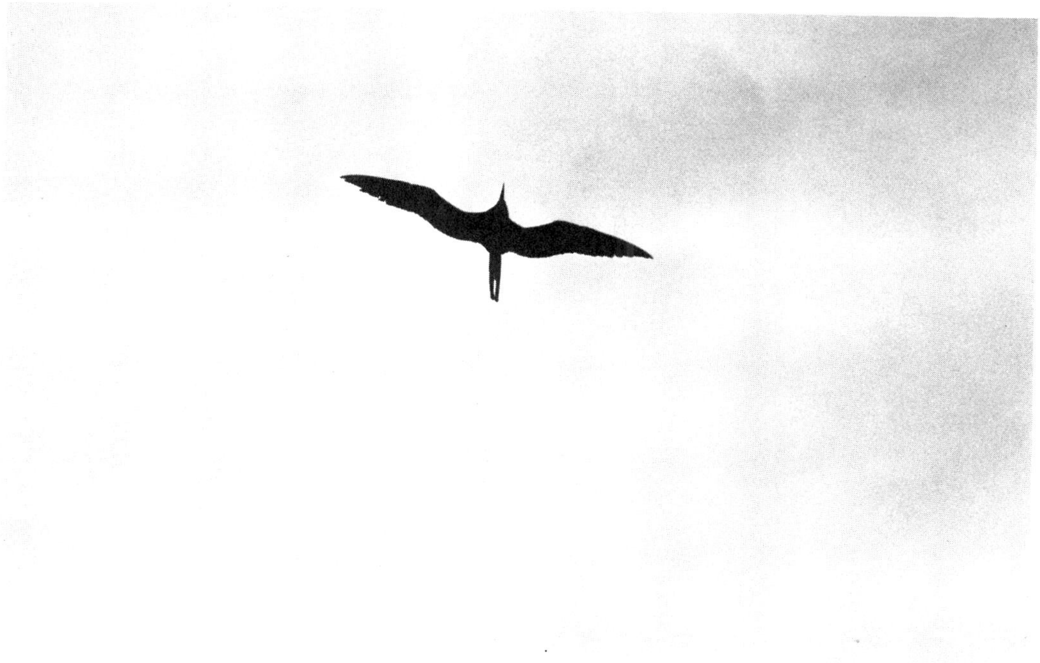

You might see more rare species flying overhead, but unless you have a powerful telephoto lens, a bird in flight will be nothing more than a silhouette against the sky. Still, a shot of a frigate bird would be an unusual and valuable addition to your video movie.

In the wild, it's another story. As mentioned earlier, use a shooter's trick to get steady video images: take a deep breath, let it all out, wait a second, and then shoot. Shooting videos of animals is in many ways like hunting without a gun. The camera is your gun, and you're hunting the images of the game rather than the game itself. The rest is the same. You have to hone your skills of patience, stealth, observation, and caution to get the best videos of animals in their natural habitat.

The essential requirement for good wildlife videos has to be patience. Without it, you won't even see the elusive wildlife you're after, much less get close enough to videotape it. Professional wildlife photographers all have one thing in common: the patience (and dedication) to wait out an animal or bird until it no longer feels threatened by human presence. The fleeting image of a leaping leopard or the airborne strike of a falcon might have been the result of days or even weeks of quiet waiting for the right moment. This is beyond a reasonable possibility for most amateurs, but it's worth knowing how the professionals get their pictures. Technically, the scenes they shoot are not that much more difficult than those you create yourself. Time is the major difference.

If you become seriously interested in wildlife videography, you'll want to consider more accessories, starting with a big lens, powerful lights for night work, remote operating controls including remote timing devices, and some place of concealment, such as a constructed blind or tree platform. That's for serious work. On the simpler side, it's comforting to know that today's lenses are at least strong enough to capture common backyard creatures and shore birds, as well as those found in the zoo. As I mentioned before, the equipment is only getting better. Regardless of what pieces you add, the emphasis in this kind of video work is on patience, stealth, and telephoto lenses.

CHAPTER FIVE

Introduction to Editing

When the shooting is finished, another form of creativity takes over: *editing*. Postproduction editing is really an extension of shooting video. It's the process of completing the vision you first had when you decided to record an event on videotape. The story line you produced, the scenes you shot, and all the decisions you made while editing with the camera come before you now like pieces of an electronic jigsaw puzzle. You know in your mind the picture you want to produce; all that remains is putting the pieces together.

Video editing is a skill bordering on art, and it's quite different from the basic requirements of shooting video. As in all photography, the eye behind the camera is not always the same as the eye of the editor. As the editor, you'll now view the recorded scenes in a different way. You might like what you shot, you might not. If you don't, you might be able to go back and shoot additional scenes, depending on the situation.

Postproduction editing is a time-consuming and precise process. You might decide not to spend any additional time editing, content instead to hold your videos in their original form and to view the entire tape or segments of it as your whim dictates. This is your choice, and it's valid.

This is very much like the way people handle their photos once they've been processed by the local film lab. Some people carefully cull the bad pictures and arrange the good shots in a pleasing sequence in photo albums or slide trays. Labeling the pictures, adding captions, and even creating slide shows are advanced projects these organized and motivated people take on. For them, organizing a good show is part of the fun and rationale for taking the pictures in the first place.

At the other end of this behavioral spectrum are those folks who look over the batch of photos and then return them to the envelopes they arrived in. Weeks, months, or even years later, they pull out the photos to refresh their memories of the pleasures of a family outing or vacation trip. If they wait long enough, they might even have the fun of trying to figure out when the photos were taken . . . where . . . and who all those people are.

The point is, both groups enjoy their pictures. One group just likes the editing process and wants to spend time doing it.

EDITING TECHNIQUES

There are basically two editing techniques: assemble editing and insert editing. *Assemble editing* involves selecting a number of scenes recorded on one tape and adding, or assembling, them in the desired sequence on a second tape. Most home editing is done by assemble editing. All you really need to do it is your video camera, the VCR you have at home (probably a VHS model), and your television.

The second editing technique, called *insert editing*, enables you to insert a scene into the middle of a previously recorded tape. This is a more complex procedure than assemble editing, but it's a nice feature to have when you want to substitute one scene for another on a tape you've already edited. Assemble editing is the norm, but an insert-edit switch on an editing VCR expands your options. Most better quality editing VCRs have this capability. Incidentally, a good video camera enables you to insert-edit over original footage in the camera. Flying erase heads are essential for this.

THE EDITING PROCESS

So you've shot your video and you're eager to take the editing challenge to transform your raw footage into a polished production. Regardless of the sophistication of your current editing equipment, you should approach the editing process in the same way: log the scenes in the tape you shot, decide on the final order of scenes, and then use all that equipment to make your vision a reality.

Logging Your Videotape

The first step in postproduction editing is to make a list of the scenes you recorded so that you know exactly what you have to work with. Get a notepad and a couple of sharp pencils. Connect your video camera or VCR to your television set and prepare for a few hours of reviewing every foot of the video you shot. On the notepad, list each scene in sequence, along with start and stop reference points (usually the footage or time measures as indicated on the tape counter) and any comments you have.

As you view the tape, think not only about which scenes to keep, but perhaps more important, which scenes to cut. First to land on the cutting-room floor are shaky images, scenes that are out of focus, and shots that are over- or underexposed. Next to be cut are those scenes or images that don't really add to your story. The point of the whole editing process, after all, is to tell an interesting story in a reasonable amount of time.

Your log sheet might look something like this:

Family Ski Trip: Tape 1

Start	Stop	Scene	Description	Comments
000	023	1	Adjusting shots	Don't use
023	060	2	Kids looking out car window	OK
060	075	3	View out window	Bad reflection
075	078	4	Shot of floor	Don't use
078	100	5	View out window	Good scene
100	110	6	Close-up of thermometer	Good cutting shot
110	150	7	View of mountain	Pan too fast; use from 130–145
150	175	8	Dad gets skis on	OK
175	225	9	Mom gliding down slope	OK; add some rousing music
225	240	10	Mom takes a fall	Funny shot; good action
240	250	11	Kids laughing	OK
250	275	12	Mom getting up and joking about her technique	OK
275	300	13	Mom skiing again	Too long; shaky start to 285
300	330	14	Dad & kids on chairlift	Needs cutting shot
330	400	15	Packing up car; skis on top	Too long; needs better sound

Yes, logging your videotapes is a tedious job, but it's a good thing to do even if you don't ever actually edit the tapes. A log sheet can help you find a sequence or two that you might want to look at later just for fun.

If you do intend to edit your work, this is the time to retrieve those 3 x 5 index cards you made when you first planned your video. Look at them while you log the tape. See if the scenes you initially outlined are similar to the ones you actually shot. If they are, keep them and then make up a few more cards summarizing all the scenes you have on tape. Use the tape counter to develop a cross-reference list so your cards correspond to the entries on your log sheet. By arranging and rearranging the index cards into a workable and coherent order, you effectively pre-edit the tape. The cards give you the skeleton of your finished work, and that structure can make your life at the editing table much easier. It's also kinder on the videotapes and the VCR playback heads than constantly running them forward and backward to find certain scenes. Shuffle the cards instead. Then make up a detailed editing plan.

The last step before doing the actual editing is to make a duplicate copy of your tape. This way, you can practice editing without wearing out or losing portions of the original tape, and you'll get a better feel for the process. Then, after you've practiced, you can make the real editing decisions much more quickly.

Walking Through a Simple Edit

For a simple edit, you need your video camera (or another VCR to play the prerecorded tape), two cassettes of videotape (one with the recorded images and the other blank), a dubbing VCR (your home VHS VCR will do for a start), a TV set equipped with audio and video input connections, and cables to hook everything together. The editing process for this setup is relatively easy.

You begin by connecting your camera to the VCR, which in turn you connect to the TV set. Now let's do a simple assemble edit. Play the prerecorded tape with your video camera and stop it when you reach the first scene you want to appear in the finished version. (You can watch the whole process on the TV monitor.) Now simultaneously press the play switch on the camera *and* the start and record switches on the VCR. When you reach the end of the first sequence you have selected for your finished tape, simultaneously stop both machines.

For the cleanest editing cuts, use the pause switch on the camera and the VCR rather than the off or stop switches. Holding the tape in pause keeps it aligned with the playback and recording heads, which reduces the chances of its reengaging out of position. Even if your equipment has flying erase heads, using the pause switch prevents the extraneous video interference that often appears on home-edited videos. This interference shows up as a quick rainbow flash of color, called a *moiré effect.* It happens when old video signals bleed through to the new video scene.

To add the next scene, just repeat the process: Play, fast-forward, and rewind the prerecorded tape until you reach the desired scene and then record it on the VCR. Through trial and error, you'll eventually wind up with an edited video movie—that is, unless you inadvertently push the wrong record button and erase your original material. If that happens and you don't have an extra copy of the original tape, be philosophical. At least you've gained experience and improved your eye-hand coordination.

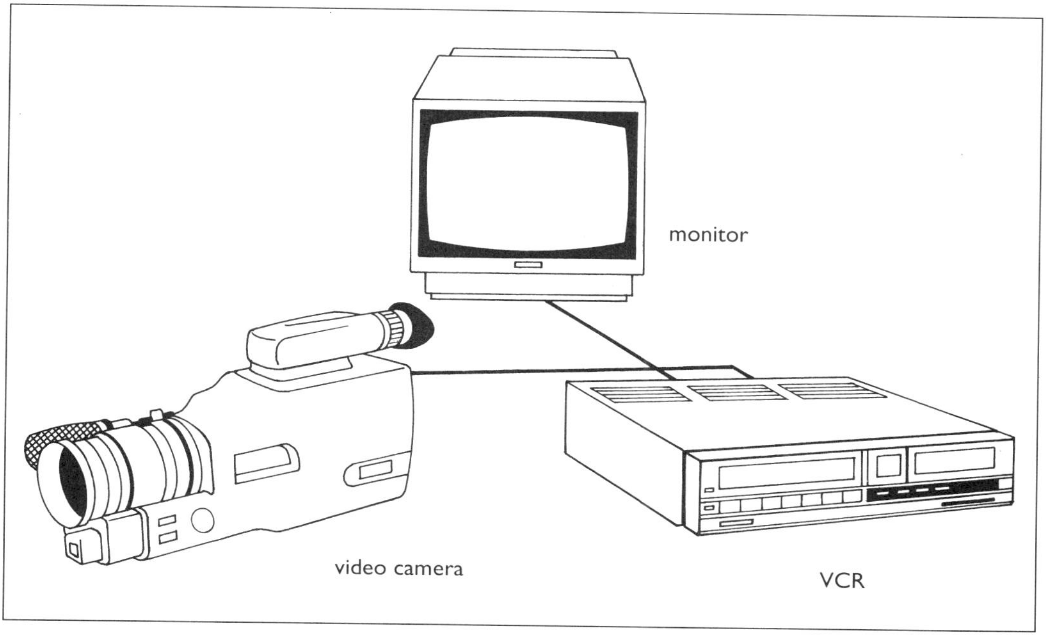

After making a list of the scenes you want to keep and noting the order in which you want them to appear, set up your equipment as shown here to do basic assemble editing. This setup is similar to that for making a copy of a videotape (of any format) using an ordinary VHS VCR. Although the quality of the second-generation tape will always be inferior to the original, you can minimize these effects by setting your VCR to SP (standard play)—the highest-quality recording mode for VHS VCRs.

As your skill at the editing table improves, you'll soon be frustrated by the limitations of your equipment. The tape transport controls on most video cameras are not precise enough to enable you to find specific points in the tape for editing, and the controls on a typical VCR are no better. Your edited tapes, while an improvement over raw footage, don't look at all professional. Indeed, if your VCR doesn't have flying erase heads (which is entirely possible), you'll see those dreaded glitches (rainbows, swirls, and video noise) between scenes. When your dissatisfaction grows extreme, it's time for some more serious and expensive equipment.

EDITING EQUIPMENT

If you move inexorably toward serious postproduction editing, you'll need some specialized equipment. The first pieces you buy will be an editing VCR and an edit controller. Later you might want to consider a video processor.

The Editing VCR

In the electronics supermarkets, VCRs are displayed in bewildering quantities and styles, each with its own features and advantages. No two are alike, and the features advanced on one model one year might not be included the next year. It's truly a puzzle for the consumer seeking easy editing answers.

The basic controls you need for the *editing VCR* include start, stop, pause, record, fast forward, reverse, review, and a counter to keep track of how much tape has passed the heads. Important features of this VCR include additional recording and playback heads, audio-mixing capabilities for multiple sound sources, input jacks for recording separate audio or video signals, an insert-edit capability, and, perhaps the most important feature, flying erase heads to provide glitch-free starts and stops so your editing is smoother.

All VCRs use two heads to record and play back videotape, but the better machines add two more heads so that you can take advantage of special features such as pause, slow motion, and double-frame advance. The extra heads mean clearer pictures when you record and play back a tape.

For more precise control over the starting and stopping points of the scenes you're editing than you can achieve with the forward, rewind, and play buttons, a jog-shuttle knob is the answer. Look for a large, manually tuned knob on the front of the deck. There's no substitute for this fine manual control when you want precise start and stop points.

There are two more features you should look for in an editing VCR: *audio dub* and *video dub*. Most basic VCRs have only one recording switch. When you activate the switch, you record everything: audio, video, and control signals. You can't split it up. But what if you want to keep the sound, but add new sections of video

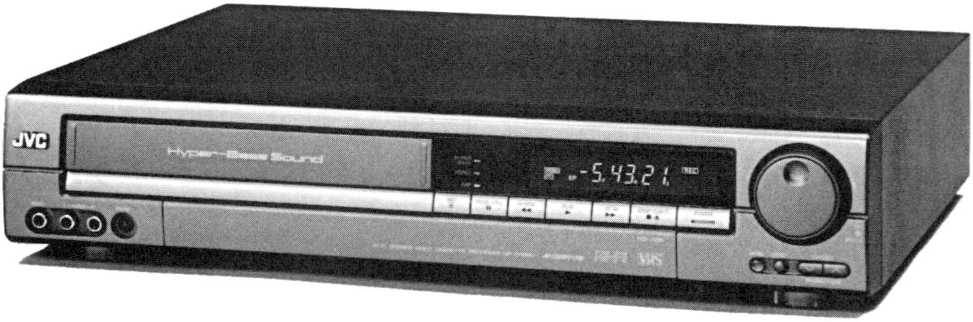

An editing VCR's jog-shuttle knob, which moves the videotape backward and forward in small increments, enables you to fine-tune your editing. (Courtesy JVC)

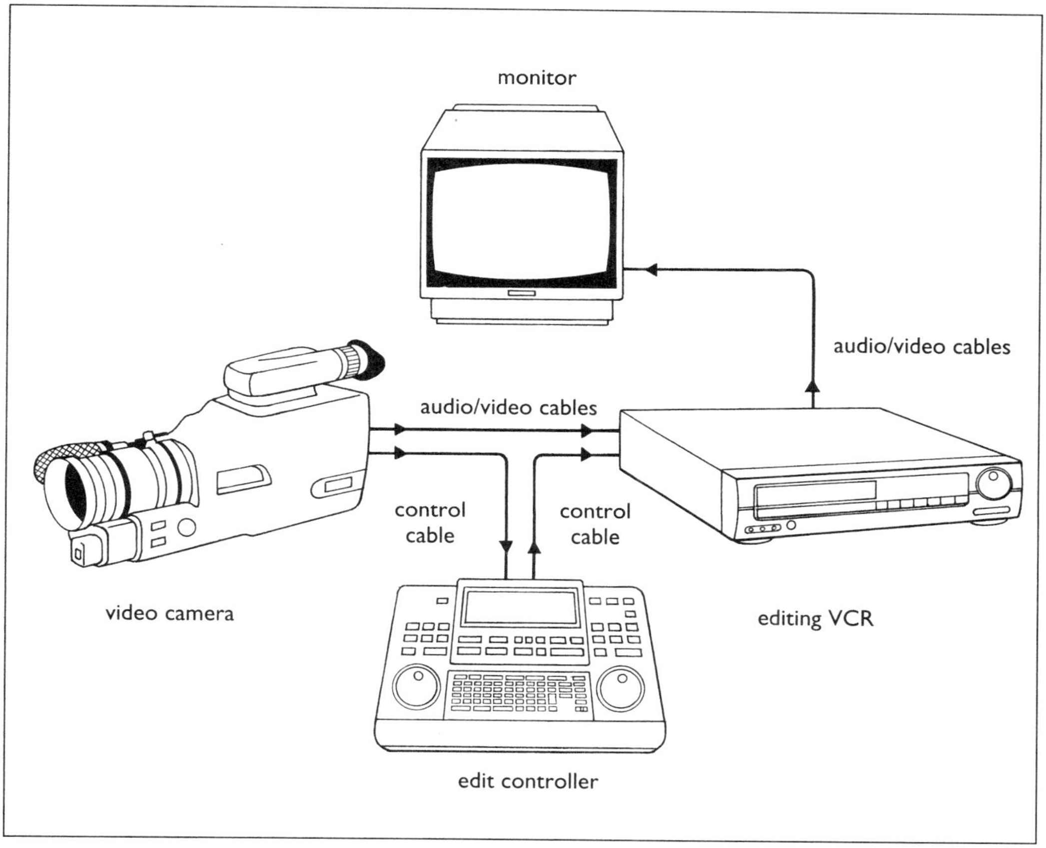

By combining an edit controller with two VCRs (or your camera and an editing VCR) you can simplify and enhance your editing technique. Just program the edit controller to record scenes from your original tape, in any order, and it will assemble them on a blank tape. Sophisticated edit controllers enable you to fade from one scene to another.

material, or move completed scenes around to make up new sequences? Or maybe you want to replace the existing soundtrack with a new one—music or narration, perhaps. For this you need audio-dub and video-dub capabilities. Audio dub enables you to record new sound without disturbing the picture; video dub lets you add pictures without disturbing the soundtrack.

No doubt about it, editing the audio and video portions of a tape in this way is complicated. The synchronization between scenes must be exact, sound levels must be equal, and the color and light intensity on the video portions must match. But do it right, and you'll have a video movie others will talk about long after it's over.

HEARING IS BELIEVING

The sound (audio) considerations when producing a video can be enormous. The easiest way to come up with a special soundtrack to complement your video is to make an audio dub—another recording of the entire soundtrack from the original video. Then you can record additional material on another audiotape and mix the audiotapes together on a final soundtrack.

You'll need a script for the sound you want, be it narration, background music, sound effects, or the ambient sound recorded when you shot the video. Then you compare the video shooting script with the audio script and come up with a combination outline in which sound and picture (audio and video) match.

So now you have an outline addressing both audio and video, and you have an edited video and an edited audiotape. Now you must match video and audio and rerecord the result onto a final videotape, which in all probability is at least a third-generation tape. That probably means you'll need to boost the signal with a video processor, so we're getting into the big league of audio/video equipment, with price tags to match. With time and a lot of patience, though, not to mention the extra equipment, you'll eventually get a nice video with a matching, coherent soundtrack.

But don't think you have to go overboard with fancy, expensive equipment to get a good finished product. For the beginner, the best editing is done in the camera at the time of shooting. This means careful preparation, a good shooting outline, possibly a script for narration, and the discipline to know when not to talk and when to allow the normal background sounds to tell the story. If you do this, even roughly, you'll have a presentable video to show to friends and family without further postproduction editing of audio or video material.

The Edit Controller

To do assemble editing efficiently, nothing beats an *edit controller*. Even the most basic edit controllers can store in electronic memory the beginning and end positions of at least 4 to 6 segments (pricier models can hold 99 or more segments) from the prerecorded tape. You enter these points by referring to the tape counter on the video camera or VCR holding the prerecorded tape. When you have registered the segments (or the memory is full), you start both VCRs simultaneously; the edit controller automatically selects the segments in the proper order (rewinding and fast-forwarding as necessary) and rerecords, or dubs, them on the blank tape.

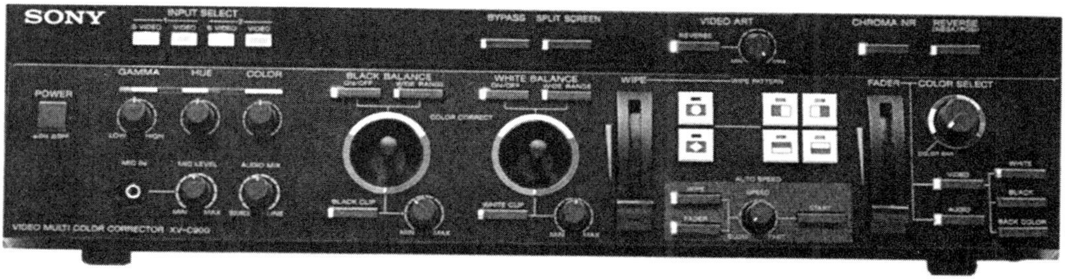

By electronically boosting signals from various playback sources, a video processor enables you to correct for color, match lighting between scenes, fade out video and audio, and add sound. (Courtesy Sony)

The Video Processor

If serious editing is in your future, there's yet another piece of equipment to consider to make the job easier: the *video processor*. There's always some loss of quality when tapes are duplicated (though it's barely discernible with S-VHS or Hi-8 tape), but the video processor alleviates it. This piece of equipment looks like a professional video control board, and it does professional-style work.

The video processor connects a variety of external audio and video sources to the editing VCR and synchronizes their inputs. It enhances both color and sound, electronically boosting the signals coming in from the various playback sources. It can also change background colors, match the colors and light intensities between scenes, enable you to fade out video and audio, and otherwise modify every kind of audio and video signal coming in from three or four different sources. You can also use it to add new sound, perhaps narration or previously recorded music. All these features improve your efforts in editing raw videotape footage into a successful finished movie.

Many quality video cameras have some of these same features, but good editing with better control is easier to accomplish *after* shooting the scenes. Regardless of the editing features built into your camera, the video processor is a marvelous tool.

Additional Editing Equipment

Two other devices you might want to consider are the character generator and the audio mixer. The *character generator* enables you to add titles or captions to the videotape by means of a keyboard. Some video cameras are equipped with a simple character generator, but stand-alone units offer a variety of type styles, sizes, and colors to choose from.

An *audio mixer* (available with either mono or stereo capabilities) enables you to add soundtracks, such as music or narration, to your edited videotape. Inserted between your video camera and your dubbing, or editing, VCR, the audio mixer intercepts the soundtrack from the original tape and can add other sound to it before passing it along to the dubbed tape. The best models have four channels with inputs for the microphone, the original sound on the tape, and two other sound sources. This is a handy piece of equipment because when you rearrange the order of scenes in your video, the recorded soundtrack might become disjointed. The ability to add a new soundtrack—complete with narration, music, and sound effects—helps ensure an exciting finished product. A top-of-the-line video processor will include these audio features.

Compatibility

You'll most likely achieve the best editing results if all your equipment is from the same manufacturer. All models vary slightly in the amount of time that elapses after you press the start button before beginning to roll the tape. Models from the same manufacturer are more likely to be synchronized than models from different manufacturers. The time delay is only about ⅙ of a second, though, so it needn't be a grave concern to most home videographers. As you become more adept, you might find you need that extra bit of accuracy. It only takes a little success before the editing bug bites and you want to try more advanced editing techniques. Remember, you're limited only by your own imagination and creativity.

THE HOME COMPUTER CONNECTION

An exciting new technology has revolutionized the field of postproduction editing. AT&T introduced software capable of editing S-VHS videotape on your home Macintosh computer. This easy-to-use system can not only isolate scenes to the exact frame, it can add in graphics you create through other Macintosh utilities. The price on this package is a bit steep (almost $1,500), but prices on new technology always come down quickly once competition enters the picture.

Another company is introducing a similar software program for use with 8mm tape and an IBM-compatible computer running Microsoft Windows. The screen displays typical VCR controls that you work by means of a mouse. Click the beginning and ending of each scene, give each a name, decide on the order of scenes, and the program does the rest. This package is well within the means of most home video moviemakers (about $200). If you already have the hardware, you might enjoy combining two hobbies into one.

TAKING CARE OF VIDEOTAPES

I can't end this chapter without giving you some advice on taking care of your videotapes. During the editing process, you'll start, stop, and rewind your tapes over and over again. Even though videotape is reasonably strong, it can be damaged. When you use the pause switch, be careful not to hold the tape in that position for long. The tape stretches while the playback heads continue to spin. This also creates friction, which eventually wears down the tape. By planning your editing sequences in advance, you lessen the risk of this happening because you don't have to make major decisions while holding the tape in pause.

The same holds true for running tapes in fast forward or reverse while the playback heads are engaged. Doing so wears down the heads as well as the tape. There is little reason to do this, except for laziness, and you'll quickly pay for it. Avoid problems stemming from this common practice by first stopping the tape (disengaging it from the heads) and then using the fast forward or reverse switches. You can use the tape counter and your log sheet or 3 x 5 cards as a guide to how far you want to go in either direction.

When you've finished with your tapes, store them in a cool, dark, dry place. Stand them upright and label them so you know what's contained on each. Avoid jarring or dropping the tapes. The tapes are magnetically sensitive, and the images can be degraded or even lost with careless handling. Don't be rough with your other video equipment either. Even solid-state electronics can be damaged or broken. Above all, don't touch the videotape itself or disturb the protective gate on the cassette. Retail stores sell tapes, but they don't repair them. These cautions notwithstanding, if you handle your tapes with care, and make periodic copies with a video processor, your tapes will keep their high quality and be viewable for many years to come.

CHAPTER SIX

A Final Review

A good video movie has a purpose and tells a story in a logical fashion. This is another way of saying that a good video has continuity, not only in the picture sequences but also in the sound. Sound continuity can come from the underlying sound track recorded when the video was shot—the ambient sound—or it can come from another source. Voice-over narration or background music both provide drama and impact to the production.

Video continuity comes from preserving the basic story line, which leads the viewer along a carefully prepared path, faithfully following the action without interruption by unrelated scenes that have been allowed to slip in. Video continuity also means consistency in light, whether the illumination is from the sun or artificial lights. The same scene, shot at different times of day, will have different light falling on it, and this will be recorded by the camera to the distraction of your audience. The light must remain the same until the scene changes markedly.

This emphasis on continuity doesn't mean a video has to be static, without variations. Camera angles can vary and the distances between the camera and the subject should change. Close-up shots can be mixed with long-distance shots; a wide-angle view can be used to set up a telephoto shot. A cutting shot can be inserted to smooth the flow of the story or to speed up action that might otherwise take too long. The cutting shot also enables you to break one scene to introduce another. Continuing to tell a coherent story is what makes creative video shooting so challenging and so effective.

LOOK FOR SIMILARITIES

Although the specific nature of the action in your videos will differ, the way you handle that action should be the same. You would videotape a downhill skier slicing through slalom gates in much the same way you would tape a waterskier carving tight turns behind a speeding boat. You would have to think about the direction and intensity of the sun, the amount of glare reflected from the water or the snow, the speed of the subject, and, perhaps the prime consideration, your own position relative to the subject.

Look at sailboats or sailboards, eagles in flight, or sail planes soaring over the mountains with a consistent eye. Don't ponder the differences; look for the similarities and realize that what you learn about making videos of one activity can be applied to another. That's the real secret behind good videos: don't leave behind what you already know.

Winter's sun and other weather conditions are the same whether you are skiing, skating, or snowshoeing. Shadows in the forest won't be different just because you're on skis rather than on a sled or a toboggan. At the beach in summer, the sand reflects a warm, even, golden light, while the sea and sky project varying shades of blue. That's the nature of the summer sun, and it appears the same whether you're fishing, boating, or building sand castles at the water's edge.

We know also that some of the physical movements and elements of drama found in one activity can have familiar counterparts in other activities. The rules of various games might differ, but the pageantry, settings, and much of the action can be remarkably similar. The same is true of video production. The techniques used successfully in one video adventure can often be applied to another. There might be some specific differences to consider, some situations unique to particular activities, but these exceptions only prove the axiom that the more things change, the more they stay the same.

GO WHERE THE ACTION GOES

People and animals videotaped in a natural setting are free to move about, and they rarely wind up in the most convenient spot for the camera. This mobility presents additional problems for the videographer, and adjustments must be made. In either instance, you must be willing and able to change your position and to vary your camera angles to find the best vantage point. And if that location lacks a solid support for your camera, you'll have to improvise a platform of sorts. Whatever you can do to steady the camera while shooting will pay dividends in the final viewing.

If you're taping birds or animals outdoors, it's vital to intrude as little as possible. You might even need some sort of camouflaged shelter or a blind to remain hidden from the wildlife. You should also know about their habits so you can be in the right place at the right time.

SPECTATOR SPORTS

Video technique changes only minimally when taping various spectator sports. All these games have a number of things in common. There's a field of play, usually some area where fans are seated, and benches for the players on the sidelines, to mention but a few similarities. Once you accommodate for what I like to call the "constant" variables (weather conditions, including light and shadows), making a video of any game should be easy, as long as you know the rules of the game itself. That's really the only variable you'll need to consider. If that seems peculiar, think about football, soccer, and rugby. All have large numbers of players running around an athletic field chasing a ball. The setting of each is almost identical. The dimensions of the playing fields differ, but the physical challenges are basically the same. The biggest difference is in how the game is played, which affects how you record it.

Of the three, American football is the most structured, the most static, and the most predictable. It also offers the most varied ways to score points. Since most sequences leading to a score are relatively obvious, though, you can usually anticipate when key moments begin to unfold and be ready to start taping. It's easy to record just a few plays and then develop a summary of action that will illustrate the entire game. You see examples of this on television every weekend during football season.

International soccer, on the other hand, is a much more freewheeling sport with sweeping action taking place rapidly from one end of the playing field to the other. Because of the nature of the game, which places a premium on defense, there is little scoring; the almost ritualistic penalty shot often determines the outcome of the contest. Penalty shots, like the more controlled football plays, can be anticipated and easily recorded on videotape. The game, while freewheeling, also has strict rules, so serious violations halt play temporarily. This enables you to get in position with your camera for a meaningful video sequence.

Rugby is more challenging still. Fans and detractors alike have called rugby "organized mayhem." There are a few rules, but they seem to have been designed not to get in the way of the action. To make a video of a rugby match, you must be very mobile and be willing to get up close to the play, because the vortex of a rugby scrum, like a tornado, is where the real action is.

Baseball has its own excitement and drama, but in this sport, the emphasis is on the individual contest between batter and pitcher. Your video work will center on these two players, and only if the batter does his job will you have reason to bring other players into the scene. Baseball has another facet that makes it unusual in team spectator sports. It's governed by innings, not time, and the games have been known to last well over five hours because there are no tie scores in baseball; extra innings determine the winner. When confronted with this situation, you'll need to figure a way around the visual tedium in your video.

So you can see that almost all spectator sports have many aspects in common when it comes to recording them. Once you understand the principles of video shooting techniques, you can concentrate on the changing environmental conditions that affect your work. If you also know the rules governing the sport, shooting the game will be that much easier.

PARTICIPATORY SPORTS

Formal rules aren't as important in participatory sports, the games we play for ourselves. Because the emphasis is not so much on how the games are played, but more on the personalities of the players themselves, you can forget the rules of the game as long as you remember the video techniques outlined in the preceding chapters. Whether you're at the beach, in a boat, on the golf course, or on the tennis courts, remember to keep the sun behind you whenever possible, watch out for glare and harsh reflections, allow sufficient time at the beginning and close of each scene, and adjust the shutter speed if it produces the effects you want. Brace the camera securely to guard against unnecessary shaking or jiggling. In short, do all the things outlined earlier, and you'll have a good video. The bonus comes as your videos continually improve, regardless of which sport you cover.

EPILOGUE

Take Time to Play

In an interview for *Vanity Fair* magazine, photographer Annie Leibovitz summarized the creative process this way: "Decisions must be made fast. I always think, What does this picture mean? Where's the best place to put my camera? Do I have anything extra in the picture, things in the background that will distract? Am I in the best position to get the essential things for this picture but no more? What is the best way to show the elements, to make a good picture, to be graphic?"

Of course, Annie was reflecting on her own highly creative work in still photography, but her approach is applicable to shooting videos. I have her words taped to the outside of my camera case, so that I see them each time I take out my camera to shoot. Answer her questions yourself whenever you shoot videos, and you'll be well on your way to having a video that not only pleases you, but delights everyone who sees your creation.

If you're like most people, the majority of the videos you shoot will be of your family and friends doing fun things together outdoors. These we've called the participatory sports. Events that are organized and staged for the benefit of an audience are the spectator sports. As the videographer, however, they're all spectator sports to you—it's your role to record other people at play. From your perspective behind the lens, the only difference between participatory sports and spectator sports is you can get closer to the participatory events.

"Hey, wait a minute," you say. "All work and no play is a bad deal. I want some fun, too!"

Here's the last tip I can offer to make shooting outdoor videos, or any videos for that matter, more fun for you. The side benefit is that you'll be improving your video skills at the same time, so this tip just might be more valuable than all the others put together.

The first step is to put your camera away, back in its case in a safe place. Now go out and enjoy the game or the sport with everyone else. Don't worry about shooting video, and don't carry your camera with you all the time, randomly scattershooting everything in sight. Enjoy your leisure activity, but also use the time to think about future videos. As you walk the open fields, take another run down the ski slopes, sink that 12-foot putt on the fourth green, or watch a goal scored in a soccer game, think about how you might shoot the scene the next time you're in that position.

Participate in your sport, learn more about it, think about your video shooting, and then shoot. Your fun will increase greatly as you begin to see new things around you. Your videos will also improve as your technical skills improve. Before you know it, your own special activity might become recording the events and actions around you. Your video camera then becomes part of you—an extra sensory device to help you perceive and retain the outside world. Now get out there and have some fun!

APPENDIX

Answers to Some Common Questions

Q: Do I need to be concerned about the videotape breaking or becoming brittle in extreme cold weather?

A: No. Videotape is generally tolerant of temperature, both heat and cold.

Q: I'm a birdwatcher and like to take videos of birds in flight, but they don't always turn out right. Either the bird is so small that you can't see it, or the picture is too dark. What am I doing wrong?

A: Try using a tight telephoto setting to get in close, and open the aperture to pull in more light. If you shoot from too far away (without telephoto), you'll be overwhelmed by the expanse of sky. Also, relying on the automatic settings in these cases causes the aperture to close down because of the brightness of the sky, making the entire picture dark. Start with a wide-angle establishing shot and then zoom in very slowly, adjusting the aperture carefully as you go. And as always, watch the results in the viewfinder and make adjustments as needed. A telephoto lens extender mounted over your zoom lens (see Chapter 2) will increase the overall lens power. Use it with some sort of camera support for a steady shot. And finally, don't rely on automatic focusing; whenever the subject is extremely small and is overwhelmed by background, the camera's sensors frantically search the scene for something to focus on and end up never focusing on anything of value. It's better in these cases to override the automatic feature and focus manually.

Q: We were driving through a national park last summer and came upon a bear foraging at the side of the road. How can I get a good shot from inside the car?

A: You're wise to stay in the car; bears (and other wild animals) might look harmless enough, but they can easily become agitated and might even charge the car. If that happens, get out of the area fast. If you're quite close to the animal, keep the windows rolled up and shoot either through the windshield or the side window. If glare is a problem, move the camera slightly to see if you can find a good angle and try to keep the lens of the camera close to the glass. If you're much farther from the animal, you can roll down your window and either lean out the car slightly or brace the camera against the side of the car. Or, if your car has a sunroof, stand on the seat and shoot from the roof (please don't do this while the car is moving).

Q: I was shooting my daughter's field-hockey game recently and thought I got some good shots. When viewing the tape later, though, I found the crowd in the background distracting. There will always be a crowd on the other side of the field, so how can I minimize the distraction?

A: Try shooting down at the action from a higher position, perhaps from higher in the stands or from the roof of a parked car (your own). Then get in close, but not too close, with the telephoto. If you get too close, you won't be able to follow the action without jerking the camera constantly this way and that. Experiment with different focal-length settings until you find one that works.

Q: I can't seem to keep my kids in one place while I'm taping them. Any suggestions?

A: Why try? Letting them act naturally will give you better results than struggling to keep them posed. You'll find they're more tolerant of doting parents, too, if you keep your distance. Incidentally, when you shoot videos of your kids, especially if they're quite young, make every effort to get down to their level. They'll feel more comfortable with the whole process than if you're looming overhead, and the perspective you get will be much more natural.

Q: Can I copy a tape from my 8mm video camera onto a blank VHS tape in my home VCR?

A: Absolutely. You can copy, or dub, a recorded tape into any other format. A Hi-8, S-VHS, or S-VHS-C tape that is copied out of the video camera onto a VHS tape will look virtually as good as the original when viewed on the typical home television.

Q: How much editing can I do to my original tape? Won't the edited version be of better viewing quality if it's original footage—not dubbed?

A: The short answer to your first question is, very little. Assuming the video camera has flying erase heads and an insert-edit feature, you can record new footage over footage already shot, though matching the length of the new scene to the one it replaces isn't going to be easy. Similarly, if the camera accepts audio dubbing, you can replace (but not augment) a portion of the original soundtrack with narration or a musical score. But you can't do any more than that without copying the tape. And yes, a dubbed tape can't maintain the quality of the original, but if the original is shot in Hi-8, S-VHS, or S-VHS-C format, the first-generation degradation is less noticeable than with standard VHS.

Q: What's the difference between the wide-angle and macro settings on a zoom?

A: One look through the viewfinder will tell you. A macro setting lets you focus on an object, say a flower, that is as close as one or two centimeters from the lens. A wide-angle setting lets you take in a wide field of vision. Their functions are very different.

Q: Does a 60mm zoom setting on a video camera provide the same magnification as a 60mm lens on a 35mm still camera?

A: No. A 60mm setting on a video camera with a ½-inch imaging chip will give roughly the same magnification as a 300mm telephoto lens on a 35mm still camera.

Q: I've heard that the tapes for an S-VHS-C video camera only give about 30 minutes of recording time at standard speed, but if you choose the extended-play feature, you can get up to 90 minutes. Is this true?

A: Yes, but with this caveat. In extended play (EP), the video and audio signals are both degraded. For the best results with *any* tape format, the standard record and playback speeds must be used. And why spend the extra money for S-VHS-C, as opposed to VHS-C, if you don't care about audio and video quality? Short playing time is the big disadvantage of VHS compact formats. This is one reason why 8mm has become so popular. The tape cartridges are roughly the same size as the S-VHS-C cartridges, yet they run about 1 to 2 hours at standard speed.

Q: Why did the colors in the sunset I taped turn out so distorted? The sky had brilliant shades of red and orange, but the tape reflected none of this.

A: Believe it or not, this is a problem of white-light balance. Whenever one color dominates a scene, the sensors in the camera assume this is incorrect and so add in the complementary color—in your case, adding blue to counteract all the red and orange. You can get more natural colors in shots of the sunset by adjusting the white-light balance on your camera. Likewise, a scene that is overwhelmingly blue might end up with a yellowish cast because the camera tried to compensate for the blue. Always adjust for white-light balance before shooting indoors or outdoors.

Q: Sometimes I need a little extra light on my subject on gloomy days, but the camera-mounted light is too harsh. Is there a middle ground?

A: Try a diffuser. A diffuser does for artificial lights what a filter does for lenses: it mutes the intensity of the light source. Placed over the light, the diffuser softens the beam and spreads it out to cover more surface area. The video camera will automatically compensate for the reduced light and adjust the exposure. By checking the image in the viewfinder, you can decide if the effect is what you're after. The diffuser is usually made of translucent plastic, or sometimes of woven cloth.

Q: What's the best way to videotape pets?

A: The most important thing is to get down to their eye level. Many photographers and videographers alike stand upright and shoot down at their subject, resulting in an awkward perspective. Either sit or lie on the ground and brace the camera securely (here's where a pocket-size tripod comes in handy). To get the animal to look in your direction, try crumpling a piece of paper. Calling the pet's name sometimes brings it running to you (any other time that would be exactly what you want). Also, try shooting from a distance and use the telephoto setting to bring the image closer. Being too close sometimes proves distracting to your pet, and you might not get the picture you're after.

Q: Last night when I turned on my backyard floodlight, I was surprised to see a big raccoon happily devouring all the seed in my bird feeder. It didn't seem bothered by the light, and I would have loved to capture that moment on videotape. Any tips for shooting through a window?

A: It's easy, especially at night with the outside floodlights on. First, turn off the indoor lights so that there's no chance of glare on the window, and so that the raccoon isn't frightened by seeing you. Then place the lens as close to the glass as possible—both for support and to keep the auto focus from honing in on the glass. Press the record button, and you have the makings of an amusing video sequence.

GLOSSARY

Amber filter—A lens filter available in various densities of amber. Used to warm a scene that is reflecting cool light.

Ambient sound—The normal sounds of the environment—whether indoors or outdoors—excluding specific dialogue, background music, and sound effects.

Aperture—The opening in a lens through which light passes to form an image. The diameter of the aperture can be adjusted to let in more or less light.

Artificial lights—Lights placed intentionally at a scene to supplement available light.

Assemble edit—An editing technique in which recorded scenes are added or copied in any desired sequence to a second videotape.

Audio—The sound portion of a recorded sequence.

Audio dub—To replace a portion of the soundtrack on the original tape with new sound; or, more commonly, to introduce new sound during postproduction editing.

Audio mixer—An editing device that enables you to include additional soundtracks on the videotape.

Audio noise—Extraneous and unwanted sound signals on the audio track. Audio noise usually consists of a hiss or a background hum.

Auto focus—A feature on video cameras in which the camera's sensors automatically focus on the nearest large image in the center of the picture.

Auto zoom—A feature on video cameras that automatically adjusts the focal length of the lens between wide-angle and telephoto positions. See also **Zoom lens**.

Available light—The light that is present in a scene without the addition of artificial lights.

Backlight—A condition in which the light source is behind the subject.

BETA—A video format that is no longer available, except on the secondhand market.

Blue filter—A lens filter available in various densities of blue. Used to cool a scene that is reflecting warm light.

Camcorder—The combination of video camera and videocassette recorder in one electronic unit. Referred to in this book by the generic term **video camera**.

Cant—Pitch of the video camera to one side or the other.

Cardioid microphone—A microphone named for the heart-shaped pattern of sound it picks up. It is most sensitive straight ahead, with the sensitivity decreasing quickly on both sides.

CCD—See **Charge-coupled device**.

Character generator—A stand-alone accessory, or a special feature on some video cameras, that enables you to superimpose titles, dates, or other characters on the videotape.

Charge-coupled device (CCD)—A semiconductor chip, typically ½-inch wide (⅓ inch in palmcorders), that is mounted behind the lens. The hundreds of thousands of silicon photodiodes on its surface receive the light from the visible image and convert it to electrical impulses that activate the magnetic coating on the videotape. Also known as an **imaging chip**.

Consistency—A principle of good composition that states that the environmental conditions in successive video sequences must match.

Continuity—A principle of good composition that refers to the action of the subject and the logical flow of events.

Cross-fade—The gradual overlapping of one picture with another. As one image begins to fade, a second image forms to become dominant.

Cutting shot—A short scene used to bridge two longer scenes. Usually different from, but related to, the main subject being taped. Also called a *cutaway shot.*

Depth of field—The area between the foreground and the background in which everything is in focus.

Direction—The implied lines of motion in the composition of a picture that leads the viewer's eye to the subject.

Dissolve—See **Fade-in/Fade-out**.

Edit controller—An electronic accessory for postproduction editing that holds a number of video sequences in memory for reassembly in a different order.

Editing—The process of reassembling audio and video material in a particular order.

Editing VCR—A video recorder with special editing features. See also **VCR**.

Fade-in/Fade-out—A technique in which the picture or sound is increased from nothing (fade-in) or decreased to nothing (fade-out). Sound is adjusted with the volume control switch; pictures are adjusted with the fade-in or fade-out switch available on some video cameras, or by opening or closing the aperture manually on cameras that permit this. Also called a **dissolve**.

Fast forward—A control on VCRs that runs the videotape forward at high speed.

Filter—A transparent or translucent fitted lens covering, usually made of glass, that modifies the quality of light passing through the lens. Filters can be of different colors and hues, or constructed to alter light waves to reduce glare or to create special visual effects.

Flying erase heads—Erase heads that are positioned on a rotating cylinder directly in line with the recording heads, which results in smooth, glitch-free edits.

Focal length—The distance from the center of a lens to the point of critical focus, measured in millimeters. Also, the measure of a lens. A telephoto lens has a long focal length; a wide-angle lens has a shorter focal length.

Format—The form or structure of a videotape.

Framing—A principle of good composition in which the subject is contained in a natural border, such as tree branches or a building corner and roof line. See also **Direction**.

Freeze-frame—A feature of video cameras and VCRs that stops and holds a single picture on the viewing screen. Used in editing to help identify the beginning and end of a particular sequence.

F-stop—A predetermined position of the aperture opening on a lens governing the amount of light allowed to pass. Lower f-stops correspond to wider aperture settings that let in more light; higher f-stops correspond to narrower settings that let in less light.

Glare—Any harsh, excessively bright light, usually sunlight or reflection.

Glitch—Electronic interference recorded on the tape, usually seen as flashes of light or bars of static. See also **Audio noise** and **Video noise**.

Head—The electromagnetic device in a VCR that transmits coded information to the magnetically sensitive tape. Two heads for audio and video material handle the basic tasks of recording and erasing; additional heads provide for special effects, such as slow motion and freeze-frame.

Hi-8—An electronically enhanced, or high-band (high-resolution), version of the 8mm video format.

Imaging chip—See **Charge-coupled device.**

Insert editing—An editing technique that enables you to insert one recorded scene in the middle of another recorded tape.

Iris diaphragm—The part of the lens that controls the amount of light passing through the lens. The setting of the iris diaphragm determines the diameter of the aperture.

Lens—An optical device that transforms light waves into visible images. See also **Normal lens, Telephoto lens, Wide-angle lens,** and **Zoom lens**.

Lens extender—A lens accessory that mounts over a video camera's zoom lens and extends the operating focal length of the lens to have more wide-angle or telephoto capability. Also called a *lens converter*.

Lens hood—A plastic or rubber accessory that shields the lens from extraneous glare and harsh side reflections. It also protects the lens from damage. Also called a *lens shade*.

Lines of horizontal resolution—A measure of quality detail in a video image. The more lines, the better the quality of picture.

Log—A detailed list of all scenes in a video sequence.

Lux—A measure of illumination. Also, the measure of the light sensitivity of video cameras. The lower the lux number, the greater the sensitivity to light.

Manual aperture—A feature on video cameras that enables you to override the automatic control and adjust the aperture of the lens according to prevailing conditions.

Manual focus—A feature on video cameras that enables you to override the automatic control and focus on selected images.

Manual zoom—A feature on video cameras that enables you to override the automatic control and adjust the focal length of the lens to suit a particular need or to do a zoom by hand.

Microphone—An electronic device that collects and changes sound waves into audible signals. Also called a *mike* or *mic.*

Moiré effect—A quick rainbow flash of color band that occurs when old video signals bleed through new pictures being recorded.

Monitor—A television set with additional audio and video input and output connections.

Monopod—See **Unipod**.

Multidirectional microphone—a microphone with a 360-degree sensitivity pattern.

Neutral-density filter—A lens filter that cuts down on excessive sunlight and glare without compromising color values. These filters are graded #2, #4, and #8, according to the degree of darkness. Also called an *ND filter.*

Nicad—Nickel-cadmium battery. A rechargeable power pack for video cameras.

Noise—Extraneous, unwanted audio or video interference affecting the clear recording of material on videotape. See also **Audio noise** and **Video noise**.

Normal lens—The standard video camera lens that most closely reproduces the picture seen by the human eye. In video, a normal lens is generally calculated between 7mm and 13mm, depending on the videotape format and the size of the imaging chip.

Panning—The sweeping side-to-side movement of the video camera while recording action or showing a broad panorama.

Picture area—The amount of screen or picture taken up by the subject.

Pixel—Picture element. A measure of electronic elements in a picture. The greater the number of pixels, the better the quality and clarity of the picture.

Polarizing filter—A lens filter that eliminates glare and reflections from harshly lighted subjects and enhances the natural colors.

Preview switch—A feature on video cameras that enables you to rewind the tape a few seconds so that you can see what was just recorded.

Refraction—The bending of light rays through a denser medium such as rain or water.

Rewind—A control on VCRs that runs the tape rapidly in reverse.

Rule of thirds—A principle of good composition in which a picture is divided into three parts, either horizontally or vertically, to produce pleasing proportions.

Shake—Unwanted camera movement.

Shotgun mike—A directional microphone used to isolate specific sounds, usually at a distance. Shaped like a long, slender cylinder.

Shutter speed—A feature on some video cameras that enables you to increase the speed of the shutter to 1/10,000 of a second or more to capture fast action.

Signal—The desired audio and video material being recorded.

Signal-to-noise ratio (SNR)—A measure of the desired signal to the unwanted noise, measured in decibels. A high ratio is preferable.

Skylight filter—A lens filter with a very slight tint. Helps cut down on unwanted glare, softens harsh light, enriches color, and protects the camera lens. Also called a **neutral-density 1-A (or 1-B) filter**.

Speed—A relative measurement of the quality of a lens calculated with the aperture at its widest position. A fast lens has a wider initial aperture setting than does a slow lens.

Start/Stop switch—A feature on video cameras that enables you to keep the camera on, but with certain functions in resting mode.

Story board—A detailed list of scenes to be shot or edited.

Supplementary lighting—Additional lighting—usually artificial—to supplement the available light.

S-VHS—An electronically enhanced, or high-band (high-resolution), version of the VHS video format.

S-VHS-C—An electronically enhanced, or high-band (high-resolution), version of the compact VHS video format.

Tape transport system—The mechanical components of a VCR, including the record and playback heads.

Telephoto lens—A lens with a long focal length designed to magnify distant images.

Tilt—The up-and-down movement of a video camera.

Tripod—A three-legged device used to support the video camera.

Unipod—A one-legged device used to support the video camera.

Variable shutter speed—A feature on video cameras that enables you to adjust the shutter speed manually.

VCR—See **Videocassette recorder**.

VHS—A ½-inch-wide videotape format. VHS stands for Video Home System.

VHS-C—The compact version of the VHS format.

Video—The picture portion of a complete videotape sequence.

Video camera—The combination of camera and videocassette recorder in one unit. Also called a **camcorder**.

Videocassette recorder (VCR)—A device that records and plays back videotapes. See also **Editing VCR**.

Video dub—To add pictures from one videotape to another without disturbing the soundtrack.

Video noise—Extraneous and unwanted picture signals showing up as snowy spots, scratches, or wavy lines. See also **Glitch** and **Moiré effect**.

Video processor—An accessory for postproduction editing that can modify audio and video signals, change color intensity, add background colors, and provide video and audio fades and other special effects.

Video 8—A videotape format identified by its overall width of 8 millimeters. Commonly called **8mm**.

Viewfinder—The viewing screen on the video camera. Similar to a tiny television screen.

White light—The apparent natural light visible to the human eye.

White-light balance—A standard of light quality equal to that perceived by the human eye. White-light balance can be corrected manually or automatically on good cameras.

Wide-angle lens—A lens having a short focal length that allows for a wide field of view.

Wind sock—a foam-rubber covering for a microphone intended to lessen wind noise.

Zoom—To adjust the zoom lens to move the subject closer or farther away while everything remains in focus.

Zoom lens—A lens having adjustable focal lengths covering all positions from wide angle to telephoto.

8mm—A videotape format identified by its overall width of 8 millimeters. Also called **Video 8**.

INDEX

*Page numbers set in **boldface** type refer to illustrations.*

D

E

F

M

N

O

P

R

S

W

Z